PERGAMON INTERNATIONAL LIBRARY
of Science, Technology, Engineering and Social Studies

The 1000-volume original paperback library in aid of education,
industrial training and the enjoyment of leisure

Publisher: Robert Maxwell, M.C.

AN APPROACH TO TEACHING AUTISTIC CHILDREN

THE PERGAMON TEXTBOOK
INSPECTION COPY SERVICE

An inspection copy of any book published in the Pergamon International Library will gladly
be sent to academic staff without obligation for their consideration for course adoption or
recommendation. Copies may be retained for a period of 60 days from receipt and returned if
not suitable. When a particular title is adopted or recommended for adoption for class use and
the recommendation results in a sale of 12 or more copies, the inspection copy may be retained
with our compliments. If after examination the lecturer decides that the book is not suitable
for adoption but would like to retain it for his personal library, then a discount of 10% is
allowed on the invoiced price. The publishers will be pleased to receive suggestions for
revised editions and new titles to be published in this important International Library.

Other Titles of Interest

Cross, G. R.   The Psychology of Learning: An Introduction for Students of Education

Evans, D. A. & Claiborn, V. and A.   Mental Health Issues and the Urban Poor

Francis-Williams, J.   Children with Specific Learning Difficulties, second edition

Francis-Williams, J.   Rorschach with Children

Gelfand, D. L. & Hartman, D. P.   Child Behavior Analysis and Therapy

Hutt. S. J. & Hutt, C. (ed.)   Behaviour Studies in Psychiatry

Kahn, J. H.   Human Growth and the Development of Personality, second edition

Kirman, B. H.   Mental Retardation

Liebert, R. M. *et al.*   The Early Window—Effects of Television on Children and Youth

O'Leary, K. & O'Leary, S. G.   Classroom Management: The Successful Use of Behavior Modification

Segal, S.   No Child is Ineducable

Wing, L. (ed.)   Childhood Autism, second edition

THE JOURNAL OF CHILD PSYCHOLOGY AND PSYCHIATRY AND ALLIED DISCIPLINES

Official Organ of the Association for Child Psychology and Psychiatry

Joint Editors: L. A. Hersov, The Maudsley Hospital, London

R. Maliphant, University College, London

This journal is primarily concerned with child psychology and psychiatry but recognizes that many other disciplines have an important contribution to make in furthering knowledge of the mental life and behaviour of children. Therefore, in order to promote an eventual integration, an important function of the journal is to bring together contributions of a high quality springing from different points of view in such fields as animal behaviour, anthropology, education, family studies, paediatrics, physiology and sociology.

The terms of our inspection copy service apply to all the above books. Full details of all books listed and specimen copies of journals listed will gladly be sent upon request.

AN APPROACH TO TEACHING AUTISTIC CHILDREN

Edited by
MARGARET P. EVERARD
for
The National Society for Autistic Children

PERGAMON PRESS

OXFORD · NEW YORK · TORONTO
SYDNEY · PARIS · FRANKFURT

U.K.	Pergamon Press Ltd., Headington Hill Hall, Oxford OX3 0BW, England
U.S.A.	Pergamon Press Inc., Maxwell House, Fairview Park, Elmsford, New York 10523, U.S.A.
CANADA	Pergamon of Canada Ltd., P.O. Box 9600, Don Mills M3C 2T9, Ontario, Canada
AUSTRALIA	Pergamon Press (Aust.) Pty. Ltd., 19a Boundary Street, Rushcutters Bay, N.S.W. 2011, Australia
FRANCE	Pergamon Press SARL, 24 rue des Ecoles, 75240 Paris, Cedex 05, France
WEST GERMANY	Pergamon Press GmbH, 6242 Kronberg-Taunus, Pferdstrasse 1, Frankfurt-am-Main, West Germany

First edition 1976

Library of Congress Cataloging in Publication Data

Main entry under title:

An Approach to teaching autistic children.

(Pergamon international library of science, technology, engineering and social studies)
Bibliography: p.
Includes index.
1. Autism—Addresses, essays, lectures. 2. Mentally ill children—Education—Addresses, essays, lectures.
I. Everard, Margaret P. II. National Society for Autistic Children (Gt. Brit.)
LC4165.A66 1975   371.9′2   75-34068
ISBN 0-08-019923-2 Flexicover
        0-08-020895-9 hardcover

Printed in Great Britain by A. Wheaton & Co. Exeter

CONTENTS

064517

LIST OF CONTRIBUTORS

BARTAK, LAWRENCE, MA. Lecturer, Department of Child Psychiatry, Institute of Psychiatry, De Crespigny Park, London, S.E.5. (now at The Faculty of Education, Monash University, Victoria 3168, Australia)

ELGAR, SYBIL. Principal of Ealing Autistic Trust, Somerset Court, Brent Knoll, Somerset, formerly Principal of The Society School, (now The Sybil Elgar School), Ealing, London, W.5.

GOULD, JUDITH, BSc, M Phil. Member of Scientific Staff, Medical Research Council Social Psychiatry Unit, Institute of Psychiatry, De Crespigny Park, London, S.E.5.

HEMSLEY, ROSEMARY L., BSc, MSc. Research Psychologist, Institute of Psychiatry, De Crespigny Park, London, S.E.5.

HOWLIN, PATRICIA A., BA, MSc. Research Psychologist, Institute of Psychiatry, De Crespigny Park, London, S.E.5.

MASON, CHRISTINE A. Teacher in Charge, Hilda Lewis House, 579, Wickham Road, Shirley, Croydon, Surrey.

PICKERING, GEOFFREY. Principal, The Dedisham School for Austic Children, Slinfold, Horsham, Sussex.

TAYLOR, JOAN E., BA Hons Eng. Dip NCTD. Teacher of the Deaf and of Children with Language Disorders, Language Unit, Charles Burns Clinic, Queensbridge Road, Birmingham 13. (Retired)

WING, LORNA, MD, MRC Psych. Member of Scientific Staff, Medical Research Council Social Psychiatry Unit, Institute of Psychiatry, De Crespigny Park, London, S.E.5.

FOREWORD

The aim of this book is to present practical information, for teachers, parents and others who may be concerned, on methods of teaching and behaviour management which have been shown to be of value in helping autistic children and those with related handicaps. The contributors are all working with autistic children and are fully aware of the difficulties of day-to-day management problems such as temper tantrums and resistance to change, so the advice they offer is based on knowledge and common sense born of first-hand experience. The book is being published in conjunction with the second edition of *Early Childhood Autism* (edited by Lorna Wing) which deals with the more theoretical aspects of the subject.

Probably the most difficult thing for people new to this problem to understand is that not only does the handicap vary in severity, but the many features which together make up the syndrome of autism are not found in equal proportions in each child, so that it is often not realized that the children have anything in common. At one extreme there is the child who is able to attend a school for normal children. He may show great ability in one or two special subjects such as music or mathematics, though, on leaving the structured environment of school, such a child may, because of his social naivety perhaps, have difficulty in holding down a job. In these children the nature of the handicap may never be recognized, although they may be considered eccentric or different from others. At the other extreme there is the very severely handicapped child, who may have presented much the same pattern of problems as the mildly handicapped child in his preschool years, but without the marked "islets of intelligence" which can be an outstanding feature in some children. A child of this kind will never be able to lead an independent life and may never learn to understand either speech or gesture, so that he will remain completely cut off from others. Most of the children fall between these two extremes, although there is a weighting towards the more severely handicapped.

To make matters even more complicated autism can be allied with deafness, epilepsy, spasticity and other handicaps. For these reasons, only general guidance can be given; each child has to be observed and assessed in order to discuss the nature of the main problems and the degree of severity of the impairments. The approach must be flexible and tailored to suit the needs of each individual child.

Once it is recognized that the basic problem lies in the lack of ability to understand what is happening around him and a difficulty in communicating flexibibly and creatively, it is not hard to see that the children, who seem so very different on first acquaintance, have this impairment in common. It is then possible to plan a programme of education and management, realistically adjusting one's aims to the potential of the child. Even in an area where expert advice is not available, the perceptive parent or teacher can do a great deal once the problem is understood. It is hoped that this book will help to achieve this understanding and also to give useful guidance on coping with day-to-day problems.

CHAPTER 1

PROBLEMS OF DIAGNOSIS AND CLASSIFICATION

LORNA WING

Definition of Terms

There is often a confusion over the use of the terms "childhood autism" and "childhood psychosis". Ideas vary widely as to what a "psychosis" really is. In the field of child psychiatry the most practical way of using the term which avoids complicated theoretical interpretations is to apply it to children whose behaviour is continually strange and unpredictable in the light of their *mental* age. There are many different patterns of behaviour which can all be included under the general category of childhood psychosis. Childhood autism is one of these patterns (or syndromes) which has been studied in more detail than any of the others.

Prevalence

Estimates of the number of autistic children vary depending on the definition used but the most extensive and most detailed epidemiological study was done in Middlesex by Lotter (1966) who found that, among children aged 8, 9 and 10, there were between 4 and 5 autistic children per 10,000. A study in Aarhus in Denmark which used similar methods produced the same result (Brask, 1970).

Boys are affected more often than girls. Again the ratio found depends on the definition used but some authors have found that boys outnumber girls by 3 or 4 to 1 (Rimland, 1964).

Many authors have said that parents of autistic children are much more likely to be middle class and professionally qualified than the average population (Kanner, 1973; Wing *et al.*, 1967). There is still controversy on this point and, yet again, the findings may be related to the definition of childhood autism that is used.

The autistic behaviour pattern begins from birth or within the first 3 years of life. Children may develop psychotic behaviour after 3 years of age but the pattern shown is not that of childhood autism.

The First Identification of the Autistic Syndrome

The autistic behaviour pattern was first identified by Leo Kanner, an American child psychiatrist, who named the syndrome "early infantile autism". His original paper (Kanner, 1943) gave a detailed and most graphic description of the abnormal behaviour of 11 children. Having described the children he then summarized what he thought were the essential features of the syndrome as follows:

1. A profound withdrawal from contact with people.
2. An obsessive desire for the preservation of sameness.
3. A skilful and even affectionate relationship to objects.
4. The retention of an intelligent and pensive physiognomy and good cognitive potential manifested, in those who could speak, in feats of memory and, in the mute children, in their facility with performance tests, especially the Seguin form board.
5. Mutism, or the kind of language that does not seem intended to serve inter-personal communication.

Problems in Making a Diagnosis

This description may sound quite clear in theory, but in practice it is difficult to apply for a number of reasons. First of all, it has not as yet been possible to show any one specific pathology of brain structure or function associated with autistic behaviour and there are no physical or psychological tests which can be used to confirm the diagnosis. It is still as necessary to rely upon careful history taking and observation as it was when Kanner first published his classic descriptions.

Kanner's lengthy descriptions of his 11 children are very clear, but his short-hand summary of 5 essential points given above are difficult to apply because some of them involve inferences from behaviour and not the behaviour itself. To take just one example, one observer (probably a doctor in his clinic) may notice that a child has poor eye contact with strangers, does not greet his parents when they come into the room and covers his ears and moves away whenever spoken to. On these grounds he may say that the child has "a profound withdrawal from contact with people". Another observer (probably a teacher in her own classroom) sees that the child has some eye contact with people he is used to, and thoroughly enjoys being tickled or involved in rough-and-tumble games. The second observer may therefore conclude that point 1 in the list cannot be applied to this child.

Kanner's belief that the autistic children he saw had "good cognitive potential" because they had remarkably good memories for certain things that interested them and were able to manipulate objects with skill has also led to many difficulties of diagnosis. Since Kanner first began to work in this field ideas about intelligence have changed considerably. The naive theory that there is a single attribute of intelligence which can predict performance in all fields is clearly incorrect. Those who work with retarded children now know that it is possible to have some skills at a high level, but to be severely handicapped in others. The assessment of the current level of non-verbal functioning in a child with autistic behaviour can be done by an experienced psychologist and is a good indication of future prognosis (Rutter, 1966a). However, attempts to assess a theoretical potential intelligence as opposed to current level of functioning are fraught with difficulty and have led to such absurdities as saying that a child must be potentially of normal intelligence because he spins the most unlikely objects with great dexterity, or because he sings in perfect tune, or because he has an alert look in his eyes. Most workers nowadays agree that the autistic pattern of behaviour can be seen in children who are mentally retarded in all areas of functioning. Lotter (1967b) estimated that about 19 per cent of children with this behaviour score in the normal range on non-language dependent intelligence tests, 25 per cent score in the mildly retarded range and 56 per cent in the severely retarded range.

The autistic pattern of behaviour, in complete or partial form, may also be found in children who have other conditions affecting the central nervous system (Chess, 1971; DeMyer *et al.*, 1971; Lotter, 1966, 1967a; Rutter, 1968; Wing, 1974a). One of the commonest accompaniments is epilepsy which occurs by the time of adult life in at least 30 per cent of people who were autistic as children (Rutter, Bartak and Newman, 1971). Some workers try to limit the diagnosis of autism to those children without additional neurological abnormalities but in practice it is impossible to apply this criterion reliably. Children diagnosed as classically autistic when young may be found to have neurological abnormalities (especially epilepsy) which do not manifest themselves until late childhood or early adult life. Some of the behaviour that is characteristic of the syndrome, particularly the language problems and the odd responses to sensory stimuli, may indicate neurological abnormalities. Current knowledge of brain function and pathology is too limited for one to be able confidently to exclude neurological abnormalities in any autistic child.

Any of the items listed by Kanner (or by other writers in the field) may occur alone without the rest, or any number may occur together without the others. It is quite likely that some items are particularly likely to cluster together (Wing, 1974a) and to merit being called "syndromes" but much more work needs to be done in this field.

Finally in this list of problems in applying Kanner's descriptions and summary of essential items, it should not be forgotten that autistic children, like all children, tend to change with increasing age. It is interesting that the two items which Kanner felt were more important than all the rest, that is withdrawal from contact with people and an obsessive desire for the preservation of sameness, are the most likely to diminish in severity as the child grows older. On the other hand, problems in using language flexibly and creatively, to be described below, improve least of all. In older children, careful history-taking is essential for making a diagnosis.

Later Work on Classification and Diagnosis

Since Kanner's original paper a great deal of work has been done in this field. In the light of the problems mentioned above it is not surprising that some of it has increased confusion rather than produced greater clarity. A number of workers (e.g. O'Gorman, 1970) have tended to widen the definition to include all kinds of children who have only minimal similarities to those described by Kanner. Those with a psycho-dynamic orientation (Bettelheim, 1967; McDougall and Lebovici, 1969), have introduced theoretical interpretations which have further confused the problems of diagnosis.

Another approach to classification has been adopted by workers who have investigated the similarities and differences between childhood autism and other handicaps such as developmental receptive speech disorders, disorders of hearing and vision and some types of mental retardation (Chess, 1971; Churchill, 1972; Pronovost *et al.*, 1966; Rutter, Bartak and Newman, 1971; Wing, 1969 and 1971).

Despite all these differing views, some writers, notably Rimland (1964) and of course Kanner himself (1973) are still of the opinion that there is a separate and distinct syndrome of childhood autism as defined by Kanner and that it is possible to make a firm diagnosis. Rimland (1971) suggests that only 10 per cent of children who are classified under the general heading of childhood psychosis have the genuine Kanner's syndrome. Most workers, however, including the present author, for the reasons described above, feel that the existence of a unitary condition of autism has not yet been proved. This does not mean that proof will not be found in the future but simply that the evidence on which to base a decision is not at present available. It seems likely that, if there is a distinct "Kanner's syndrome", it will be found among the children who function in the normal or nearly normal range in their non-language dependent skills.

Language Problems

The major point which has emerged from recent work, particularly from comparative studies, is the importance of the language impairments in autistic children. Kanner himself gave excellent descriptions of the problems his original eleven children had in comprehending and using language. Unfortunately he wrote before the development of the modern theories of linguistics, so he was unable to compare the language of autistic children with that of young normal children in the light of these theories.

Chomsky's ideas on language development are of considerable interest in this field (Brown, 1965; McNeill, 1966). He has suggested that human beings are normally born with the potential for learning the rules by which words are combined and recombined to express ideas. He points out that by 3–4 years of age normal children can use these rules to create sentences that they have never heard spoken by others. Normal people can use language flexibly and creatively either in conversation with other people or silently as "inner language". In young children the development of inner language is shown by their increasing use of imaginative play (Sheridan, 1968). In older children and adults inner language is used for thinking about past experiences and in planning for the future.

In contrast, autistic children seem to lack the potential for developing flexibility in language use. The autistic children who can speak seem to rely on rote learning of set words and phrases rather than a creative use of the basic rules. Some are able to acquire very large vocabularies and a collection of phrases and sentences. However, conversing with them is very like talking to a gramophone record or to a computer. The subjects of conversation are strictly limited and the same questions evoke the same responses with monotonous regularity. The problem extends to all types of communication such as gesture, writing and formal sign language as well as spoken speech. The autistic child therefore differs from the child with developmental receptive speech problems who cannot understand and use speech but who can communicate through gesture and mime.

This global language problem can vary greatly in severity. There are some children who are totally unable to comprehend and use any symbols at all. They are usually very severely retarded in all areas. At the other end of the scale is the autistic child with good non-verbal skills who can use grammar fairly competently but who is nevertheless unable to use his language for imaginative play, for understanding his past experience or for planning for the future. Whatever the level of severity of the impairment its presence is associated with many problems of social and cognitive development, perhaps because inability to use the rules of language *flexibly* is a special facet of a general difficulty affecting rule-using in all aspects of life. It can be suggested that the autistic child's characteristic social naivety and lack of understanding of other people's feelings is due to his inability to comprehend and use the exceedingly complex rules of social interaction which involve non-verbal even more than verbal communication.

Different degrees of impairment may well be produced by very different underlying pathologies. The important point is that all children with this type of language handicap, whatever the underlying cause, are very likely to have the autistic pattern of behaviour in partial or complete form (Wing, 1974a).

The presence of the global language impairment, whether severe, moderate or mild, has important implications for education. Whether or not the children are classically autistic, they will need the same type of structured educational programme based on an understanding of their specific handicaps. The aims of education for the severely handicapped child who has no skills at all will be very different from the child who has non-language dependent skills in the normal range, but the basic principles behind the methods used are the same.

The Practical Approach

The discussion so far has concerned issues which are of great theoretical importance for research into cause and prognosis, but the difficulties in solving the theoretical problems should not be used as an excuse for refusing to provide services for children with many or all of the features which go to make up the autistic syndrome. In practice, even if one cannot with certainty identify a nuclear syndrome of early childhood autism, it is nevertheless possible to identify specific impairments of function with sufficient accuracy to allow useful recommendations for education and management.

The most helpful way to present a diagnosis in child psychiatry is to give, separately, the type of behaviour pattern that a child shows (e.g. childhood autism), the underlying cause of his behaviour pattern if it is known (e.g. maternal rubella) his level of social and intellectual functioning as shown by appropriate tests, and any additional physical conditions which may be present (e.g. epilepsy). Important factors in the social environment should also be noted (Rutter, 1969; Wing, 1970).

For the clinician and the teacher, who have to deal with children in practical terms, the most satisfactory way of recording a child's behaviour pattern is to describe it in concrete detail rather than using short-hand labels. The Nine Points formulated by the working party chaired by Dr. Mildred Creak (1961) attempted to do this for childhood autism, but unfortunately the list contained too many theoretical interpretations of behaviour. De Myer *et al.* (1971), Rutter (1966b), J. K. Wing (1966), L. Wing (1972a) have also given detailed descriptions which have as far as possible avoided inferences.

A Scheme for Diagnosis

On the basis of recent work on the language problems and other impairments of function found in children who have autistic behaviour, or some features of the autistic pattern, it has been possible to devise a list of the characteristic impairments, special skills and behaviour problems upon which a descriptive diagnosis can be based. The list given below is a somewhat modified version of that which first appeared in *Communication*, the journal of the National Society for Autistic Children (Wing, 1972) and is an attempt to avoid the problems posed by previous diagnostic schemes. The items are described in concrete terms with a minimum of theoretical interpretation. The behaviour can be observed in the child's own familiar environment by the people who know him well.

The Handicaps of Autistic Children

A. Basic Impairments

1. *Language Problems*

   (a) Spoken language
       *(i) Problems in comprehension of speech.
       *(ii) Abnormalities in the use of speech:
           *Complete absence of speech or, in those children who do speak:
           *Immediate echolalia (a parrot-like repetition of words the child has just heard spoken).
           *Delayed echolalia (repetition of words or phrases heard in the past, often in the accent of the original speaker).
           *Repetitive, stereotyped, inflexible use of words and phrases.
           *Confusion over the use of pronouns.
           Immaturity of grammatical structure of spontaneous (not echoed) speech.
           Aphasia in spontaneous (not echoed) speech (i.e. muddling of the sequence of letters and words; confusion of words of similar sound or related meaning; problems with prepositions, conjunctions and other small linking words, etc.)
       *(iii) Poor control of pitch, volume and intonation of voice.
       (iv) Problems of pronunciation.

   (b) Non-spoken language and non-verbal communication
       *(i) Poor comprehension of the information conveyed by

---

*Items essential for a diagnosis of autism as described by Kanner (1943).

gesture, miming, facial expression, bodily posture, vocal intonation, etc.

*(ii) Lack of use of gesture, miming, facial expression, vocal intonation and bodily posture, etc., to convey information (the only "gesture" may be grabbing someone else's hand and pulling them towards a desired object).

2. *Abnormal Responses to Sensory Experiences*

(i) Abnormal response to sounds (indifference, distress, fascination).

(ii) Abnormal response to visual stimuli (indifference, distress, fascination).

(iii) Abnormal response to pain and cold (indifference, over reaction).

(iv) Abnormal response to being touched (pushing away when touched lightly but enjoying boisterous tickling and romping).

(v) "Paradoxical" responses to sensations (e.g. covering eyes in response to a sound, or ears in response to a visual stimulus).

3. *Abnormalities of Visual Inspection*

(i) The use of peripheral rather than central visual fields (responding to movement and outline rather than to details; looking past rather than at people and things).

(ii) Looking at people and things with brief rapid glances rather than a steady gaze.

4. *Problems of Motor Imitation*

(i) Difficulty in copying skilled movements (the child learns best if his limbs are moved through the necessary motions).

(ii) A tendency to muddle left/right, back/front, up/down.

---

*Items essential for a diagnosis of autism as described by Kanner (1943).

5. *Problems of Motor Control*

    (i) Jumping, flapping limbs, rocking and grimacing when excited.

    (ii) A springy tip-toe walk without appropriate swinging of the arms.

    (iii) An odd posture when standing, with head bowed, arms flexed at the elbow and hands drooping at the wrists.

    (iv) Spontaneous large movements, or fine skilled movements, or both may be clumsy in some children, though others appear to be graceful and nimble.

6. *Various Abnormalities of Autonomic Function and Physical Development, Including:*

    (i) Erratic patterns of sleeping and resistance to the effects of sedatives and hypnotics.

    (ii) Erratic patterns of eating and drinking, including consumption of large quantities of fluid.

    (iii) Lack of dizziness after spinning round.

    (iv) Immaturity of general appearance and unusual symmetry of face.

B. Special Skills (contrasting with lack of skill in other areas)

    *1. Skills that do not involve language, e.g. music, arithmetic, dismantling and assembling mechanical or electrical objects, fitting together jig saws or constructional toys.

    *2. An unusual form of memory which seems to allow the prolonged storage of items in the exact form in which they were first perceived, (e.g. phrases or whole conversations spoken by other people), poems, long lists (e.g. of all the kings of England) long passages of music, the route to a certain place, the arrangement of a collection of pebbles, the steps to be followed in a routine activity, a complicated visual pattern, etc. The items selected for storage do not appear, on any criteria used by normal people, to be of any special impor-

---

*Items essential for a diagnosis of autism as described by Kanner (1943).

tance, and they are stored without being interpreted or changed.

C. Secondary Behavior Problems

*1. Apparent aloofness and indifference to other people, especially other children, although enjoying some forms of active physical contact. Some autistic children, even under 5 years of age, show attachment, on a simple physical level, to adults they know well but are indifferent to children of their own age. N.B. This problem may diminish or disappear with increasing age though relationships with understanding adults are always much better than those with peers.

*2. Intense resistance to change and attachment to objects and routines. A fascination with regular repeated patterns of objects, sounds, routines, etc. The collection, for no apparent purpose, of objects such as plastic bottles, pebbles, knobs from biros. Older children who have a good vocabulary and some command of grammatical constructions may be fascinated by certain topics, e.g. electricity, astronomy, birds; they ask repeated questions and demand standard answers. The interest is not a creative one, but is repetitive and stereotyped in form.

3. Inappropriate emotional reactions. These include lack of fear of real danger, but excessive fear of some harmless objects or situations; laughing, weeping or screaming for no apparent reason; laughing when someone else is hurt or another child is scolded. These reactions result from lack of comprehension of the meaning of the situations.

*4. Poverty of imagination:

(a) Inability to play imaginatively with objects, toys or other children or adults; or to imitate other people's action in an imaginative, creative way. Lack of understanding of the purpose of any pursuits which do not bring an immediate and

---

*Items essential for a diagnosis of autism as described by Kanner (1943).

obvious sensory reward and of those which involve an understanding of words and their complex associations, e.g. school work, games, hobbies, social conversation, literature, poetry, etc. There is a consequent lack of motivation to indulge in these activities, even if the necessary skills are available to the child.

(b) A tendency to select for attention minor or trivial aspects of things in the environment instead of an imaginative understanding of the meaning of the whole scene, e.g. attending to one ear ring instead of a whole person, a wheel instead of the whole toy train, a switch instead of the whole piece of electrical apparatus, reacting to the needle used for an injection while ignoring the person who is giving it.

(c) Absorption in repetitive activities such as stereotyped movements, touching, tasting, smelling and manipulating objects and, sometimes, self injury.

5. Socially immature and difficult behaviour, including running away, screaming in public, biting or kicking other people, grabbing things off counters in shops, making naive and embarrassing remarks.

It is unusual to find children who have all the problems mentioned in the list. Many combinations of items in addition to the classic Kanner's syndrome will be found if a large number of children suspected of being autistic are observed. It is of intellectual interest to decide which children fit Kanner's description and which do not, but, in practice, the prescription of education depends upon the specific impairments, special skills and behaviour problems shown by the child and not upon the label that is given to him. If impairments affecting both comprehension and use of spoken and non-spoken language are present, then the type of education suitable for autistic children will be necessary, whether or not the child is classically autistic.

CHAPTER 2

ASSESSMENT: THE ROLE OF THE TEACHER

LORNA WING

As discussed in the previous chapter, children who are autistic or who show some of the items of behaviour characteristics of early childhood autism vary greatly in the severity of their handicaps and in their level of development of social and intellectual skills. It is impossible to plan a programme of behaviour management, teaching and treatment of medical problems without a detailed preliminary assessment of the child's impairments of function, behaviour problems, and, just as important, his abilities.

Ideally, assessment should be done by a multi-disciplinary team, including a child psychiatrist, a paediatric neurologist, a psychologist, a speech therapist who is interested in all aspects of language development and a social worker who knows the family, as well as the teacher. The information obtained by each of these experts should be brought together and discussed in order to form a complete picture of each child's problems and assets, leading to a plan of action.

Many teachers do not have the advantages of working within a professional team. In this case the records which a teacher can keep on her own are even more important since they can at least be used as the basis of a teaching programme.

The teacher is in the special position of being able to make extended observations of the child's behaviour because she is with him for several hours each day. The parents are with the child for even longer, but the teacher has the additional advantage of her special training which enables her to assess the child's response to her attempts to teach a variety of different skills. She also has experience of many different children and can evaluate a child's performance and progress in comparison with others in the class. In order for observations to be put to practical use they must follow an organized plan which is detailed and comprehensive.

The scheme for observing children given below draws heavily upon scales and methods of assessment which are already available, including the Vineland Scale of Social Maturity (Doll, 1965), Gunzberg's Progress Assessment Chart (1966) and Williams' and Kushlick's Structured interview schedule (1969). The work of Rutter, Bartak and their colleagues (Bartak *et al.*, 1974; Cox *et al.*, 1974), Egan *et al.* (1969), Sheridan (1969) and Wing (1969), has also been used.

The reason for presenting yet another assessment scheme when good ones are already available is that none of those in regular use is especially adapted for children with the language, cognitive and perceptual disorders found in early childhood autism. Unless a special scheme like the one below is used important facets of behaviour are not recorded. The items used here closely follow those in the M.R.C. Structured Interview Schedule of Children's Handicaps, Behaviour and Skills, which is designed as a pre-coded rating scale (Wing, 1974a,b).

Two kinds of observations are made in this scheme. One concerns the stage the child has reached on the scale of normal development and includes such items as feeding, washing and dressing. The other type of observation concerns deviations from normal development, such as echolalia, intense resistance to change, and various forms of difficult behaviour. Normal children may of course show any of these problems for a brief period, but they are not an inevitable stage of normal development in the same sense as are the steps in acquiring, for example, self care skills.

All autistic children show a mixture of developmental delay in some areas, especially language, and various deviations from normal development. It is a useful exercise to consider into which category to place each of the problems which are present in any individual child, since this has a bearing upon the choice of method for helping the child to overcome a particular difficulty. Thus, backwardness in self feeding requires a teaching programme to help him acquire the next step in the development of this skill, whereas self-injury has to be systematically discouraged while teaching more constructive activities (see later chapters).

The scheme is a lengthy one, covering many aspects of function. Unfortunately, it is not possible to reduce its length without diminishing its usefulness. Each aspect of behaviour that is covered is of relevance to the child's social and intellectual functioning and has to be considered in the teaching programme. One of the major characteristics of autistic children is the patchiness of their performance. A child can be highly competent in some things but function as severely retarded in others, so it is impossible to predict his level of skill in any one area from a knowledge of his other abilities. Therefore it is necessary to consider all the different aspects of his behaviour in a systematic way in order to pin-point problems and any compensating skills.

It should be emphasized that there is no magic short cut to the assessment of children with severe language disabilities and other cognitive and perceptual problems that is available to any of the professional workers involved. The only way to obtain a full picture of the child is to assemble each detail, piece by piece, like a jig saw puzzle. The pieces to be assembled include the results of medical and neurological examinations, performance on a variety of psychological tests and, most important of all, the way the child functions in everyday life which is covered in the standardized description given here.

Notes on Using the Assessment Scheme

When recording a child's behaviour it is important to describe what he actually does and not to give either theoretical interpretations or guesses about "hidden potential". The child's responses should be observed by setting up the appropriate situation. Thus his comprehension of speech and of gesture can be tested in the classroom by giving him instructions of varying complexity when an appropriate occasion arises. Concrete examples should be given; for example, it is more informative to note that a child climbs to the top of all the wall bars in the gymnasium with remarkable speed than simply to say that he climbs with agility. The assessment cannot be completed until the teacher has had the child in her class long enough to see how he behaves in the relevant situations. The actual length of time necessary varies with different children.

If it is not possible to say whether a certain type of behaviour is present, this should be recorded as "don't know". Sometimes "not applicable" has to be used, for example for the abnormalities of speech in children who are mute.

For each abnormality of behaviour, the frequency of its occurrence and its severity should be noted.

If required, standard forms for recording observations could be designed to suit the requirements of any individual school or unit and included in the child's case notes. If this is done, space should be left for illustrative descriptions of behaviour.

When children are living at home and attend school daily, some information, such as the pattern of sleeping, will have to be obtained from the parents. Parents can in fact use the scheme to describe the behaviour of their child at home. The contrast between home and school is always of interest and may give clues to improving methods of teaching and management in both situations.

A Standardized Scheme for Assessment

I. Language (spoken and non-spoken)

Spoken

(*a*) *Comprehension of speech*

> (i) Does the child respond to his own name? Does he point to some familiar objects when asked? Does he obey very simple instructions in a familiar context (e.g. "give me your cup"). Do you ever send him out of the room to fetch one familiar object? Could he be sent out for two or three things? Does he obey a sequence of commands "first do this, then this, then this"? Does he obey instructions needing decisions,

("if __, if not __")? Can he understand past and future tenses as well as present?

(ii) Does he have any problems with prepositions? e.g. Does he look in the right place if told "it is under the cupboard" as well as "it is *in* the cupboard".

(iii) Does he comprehend better if instructions are sung to a tune instead of spoken?

(*b*) *Use of speech*

(i) If the child does not talk, does he make any noises? Does he babble like a baby? Do his noises have a conversational intonation? Do any of his noises have a definite meaning?

(ii) If he says some words, are these just parrot-like echoing? Does he name any objects or people when asked? Does he name some things spontaneously? Does he join two words together? Does he make longer phrases but miss out the small linking words? Does he make complete sentences? Does he use past, present and future tenses?

(*c*) *Pronunciation*

(i) How clearly does the child speak? Can he be understood by people who know him well, or by strangers?

(*d*) *Intonation*

(i) Does the child use intonation to aid expression—e.g. in asking questions, in showing puzzlement, hesitation, etc., or is his intonation always the same?

(ii) Does he control the loudness and pitch of his voice?

(iii) Does he ever use a special voice, different from his usual one?

(*e*) *Echolalia*

(i) Does the child immediately repeat words or phrases spoken by other people in a parrot-like meaningless way?

(ii) Does the child repeat words or phrases used by other people some time after he has heard them? Does he talk to himself using these repeated phrases?

(*f*) *Stereotyped use of phrases*

(i) Does the child confuse pronouns, e.g. saying "you" when he means "I"?

(ii) Does the child use words and phrases in a rigid, stereotyped way, e.g. referring to something by using the word or phrase first associated with it, such as "you—paint—it" for scaffolding or "you can't have that red pot" whenever any request made by the child is refused?

(*g*) *"Aphasia"*

(i) Does the child muddle the sequence of letters in words (e.g. diccifult = difficult)?

(ii) Does the child muddle the sequence of words in sentences (e.g. Take park to dog. Put salt it on)?

(iii) Does the child confuse words that are opposites or are usually paired (e.g. on and off, yes and no, sock and shoe, mummy and daddy)?

(iv) Does the child hesitate and search for words when talking spontaneously?

Non-spoken

(*h*) *Comprehension of non-spoken communication*

(i) Does the child respond to concrete clues in the situation—e.g. does he know he is going out when he sees his coat? Does he understand pointing and beckoning? Does he respond to a simple mime such as a finger on the lips to mean "quiet"? Does he respond to complex mime such as pretending to eat, drink, brush hair, etc?

(ii) Can his behaviour be controlled by his teacher's facial expressions without using speech, e.g. by smiles or frowns? Do these have to be exaggerated for him to respond?

(iii) Does he respond to a nod or a shake of the head to mean yes or no, unaccompanied by speech?

(*i*) *Using non-spoken communication*

(i) If the child cannot speak, how does he get things he wants? Does he just scream; get everything for himself; pull other people by the hand; point by touching; point from a distance; use mime and gesture to indicate his needs; or a mixture of these methods?

(ii) Does the child have a range of facial expressions? Does he just look happy or miserable, or can he look surprised, puzzled, enquiring, etc?

(iii) Does he nod or shake his head, clearly meaning yes or no? Does he use other gestures such as "thumbs up" to indicate success or approval?

Spoken or non-spoken

(*j*) *Social communication* (by speech, gesture, miming or sign language)

(i) Does the child point things out to other people and want them to look? Does he spontaneously talk about things that have happened to him? How often does he do this and how much detail does he give? Does he tend to repeat the same things or does he tell of new things as they happen?

(ii) Does the child answer questions (by speech or by nodding and shaking of the head)? Does he do it reluctantly or willingly? Does he ever engage in a conversation? Are his contributions stereotyped and repetitious, or can he converse freely and change the subject appropriately? Does he converse about things outside his own immediate experience?

(iii) Does he ask questions? Are these limited to his own needs or does he ask questions because of curiosity? Does he ask questions about things outside his own personal experience?

Are his questions repetitive and stereotyped, or do his
questions show a creative developing interest?
(iv) Does he talk to, or otherwise communicate with children of
his own age? Does he do this reluctantly or willingly?

II. Responses to sensory stimuli

(a) *Sounds*

(i) Does the child ignore some sounds? Do some distress him? Do
some fascinate him?

(b) *Visual stimuli*

(i) How does he react to lights and shiny objects?
(ii) Does he twist and flick his hands or objects near his eyes?
(iii) Does he like to watch things spin?
(iv) Does he seem to concentrate on one aspect of an object or
person and ignore the rest, e.g. electrical switches, circular
shapes, people's teeth?
(v) Does he seem to identify things and people by their outline
rather than by the details of appearance?

(c) *Pain, heat and cold*

(i) Does the child ignore pain, heat or cold? Is he oversensitive?
(ii) Does he deliberately injure himself in any way?

(d) *Sensations of bodily movement*

(i) Does he especially enjoy rapid movement, e.g. swings, slides,
round-abouts, etc?
(ii) Does he spin himself round? Does he become giddy when he
does this?
(iii) Does he rock, jump or show other stereotyped movements?

(*e*) *Touch, taste and smell*

(i) Does he tend to explore objects and people through touch, taste and smell?

(N.B. If there is a possibility that the child may be deaf or partially sighted, the teacher's observations can provide useful evidence. It should be noted if the child responds consistently to some sounds or some visual stimuli. The nature of these stimuli and the circumstances in which the child responds should be described.)

III. Movement, gait and posture

(i) How does the child walk? Does he swing his arms? Does he walk on tip toe? Does he look odd and awkward? Is he particularly graceful in spontaneous movement?

(ii) Is he dextrous or clumsy in his fine finger movements?

(iii) Is his posture odd or awkward in any way?

(iv) Can he copy other people's movements? Does he wave good-bye? Does he clap? Are these movements easy or are they stiff and awkward? How easily does he learn gymnastic exercises, dances, miming games, etc? Does he confuse up/down, back/front, right/left when trying to copy?

(v) How does he behave when excited? Does the excitement produce movements of his whole body, including face, arms and legs?

IV. Social responses

(i) How many people could the child recognize and respond to if he met them in an unfamiliar context? No one? His parents only? His teachers? A circle of friends and neighbours?

(ii) How does the child respond to gentle touches, to cuddling, to rough-and-tumble games?

(iii) How does the child respond to social approaches without physical contact?

(iv) Does he show affection to others spontaneously?

(v) How does he respond to children of his own age as opposed to adults? Does he have any friends of his own age?

(vi) How does the child make eye contact? Does he have a blank, unfocused stare? Does he avoid making eye contact at all? Does he give brief flashing glances only? Does he stare too long at times? Is his eye contact better with people he knows than with strangers?

V. Emotional responses

(i) Does he have any special fears?

(ii) Does he seem unaware and unafraid of some real dangers?

(iii) Does he sometimes laugh or seem very distressed for no reason at all?

(iv) Does he show any response to other people's feelings, e.g. would he be sympathetic if someone had an accident? Would he be aware if someone felt miserable or ill?

VI. Resistance to change and attachment to objects and routines

(i) How does the child respond to changes in the daily routine? Does he insist upon exact repetition of some or all of the daily programme, e.g. the same route for the daily walk, everyone at the same place at table, etc?

(ii) Does he carry out rituals of his own, e.g. tapping on a chair before sitting down, touching everything on the table before eating, etc?

(iii) Does he arrange objects in special ways, e.g. in long lines or patterns? Does he replace things in the exact position from which they came, down to the smallest detail?

(iv) Is he attached to particular objects which must accompany him everywhere? How does he react if the object is lost? Does he collect any type of object in what seems to be a completely purposeless way, e.g. holly leaves, detergent packets, segments of rubber beach balls, etc?

(v) Does he have an obsessive, repetitive, uncreative, stereotyped interest in certain subjects, e.g. the planets, electricity, bodily functions, etc?

(vi) Is his play repetitive and stereotyped, e.g. does he continually manipulate the same objects in the same way; play the same record again and again; re-do the same puzzle repeatedly; perform the same series of physical actions, perhaps for hours at a time?

VII. Play and amusements

(i) How well can the child handle objects and constructional toys? Does he roll things along the floor? How many bricks can he build into a tower? Can he use screw toys? Can he do in-set puzzles or real jig saw puzzles? How many pieces? Does he make things with constructional toys? Can he follow the printed diagrams with, for example, Lego or Bilofix?

(ii) Does he have any imitative or imaginative play? Does he use real objects for their correct purpose? Does he copy his mother in domestic tasks? Does he give people pretend cups of tea in toy tea sets? Does he play with cars or trains as if they are real, e.g. putting cars into a garage, shunting the trains, etc? Does he play with toy animals or dolls as if they are real? Does he kiss them, put them to bed, hold dolls' tea parties, play school with them, etc? Does he pretend to be, e.g. a cowboy, policeman, nurse, etc., acting out an imaginary game, not just wearing the costume?

(iii) Does he play imaginatively with other children, e.g. doctors and nurses, mothers and fathers, cowboys and Indians, etc? Does he take an active part or is he always passive and not contributing to the fantasy?

(iv) Does he join in co-operative play that does not need fantasy, e.g. chasing; circle games like ring a roses; hide-and-seek; ball games played without rules; games with rules like football; table games.

(v) What types of outings does he enjoy?

(vi) What does he watch on television?

(vii) Is he interested in stories read aloud?

(viii) Does he enjoy listening to music? Can he sing in tune? Can he play any instrument?

VIII. Difficult or socially immature behaviour

(i) Does he run away or wander?

(ii) Is he destructive?

(iii) Does he scream frequently or for long periods, or have temper tantrums?

(iv) Is he aggressive to adults or to children?

(v) How does he behave in public? Does he grab things in shops; scream in the street; make naive remarks; feel people's clothing, hair or skin, etc?

(vi) Does he tend to be less active than other children, or is he overactive?

(vii) Does he resist whatever you try to do for him or automatically say no to any suggestion?

IX. Special skills found in classically autistic children

(*a*) *Non-language dependent skills*

(i) Does the child have any special skills in dismantling, assembling or manipulating mechanical or electrical objects?

(ii) Does he have any outstanding musical skill? Does he have absolute pitch?

(iii) Can he do lengthy calculations in his head?

(*b*) *Outstanding memory*

N.B. The classic autistic child remembers things exactly as they were first experienced, with little or no appreciation of their real significance.

(i) Does the child remember verbal material, e.g. poems, songs, lists of names, details of a subject which especially interests him, unusually well?

(ii) Does he notice if any object, however small or unimportant, is moved from its usual position?

(iii) Does he seem to recognize routes and places with unusual accuracy? Does he remember details of maps, etc. with unusual accuracy?

(iv) Does he remember numerical material unusually well, e.g. multiplication tables, the dates of events, days on which dates fall, train timetables, etc?

X. Self care

(*a*) *Mobility*

    (i) Can the child walk without help? Can he run as well as other children of his age?
    (ii) Can he walk upstairs and downstairs without help?
    (iii) Is he able to climb with agility?
    (iv) Can he pedal a tricycle or a bicycle?

(*b*) *Feeding*

    (i) Does he have to be fed, or can he feed himself with his fingers, a spoon, spoon and fork, or knife and fork? Can he help himself to food when at table? Can he cut a slice of bread from a loaf?
    (ii) How good are his table manners?
    (iii) Are there any problems with chewing?
    (iv) Does he dribble?
    (v) Are there any marked food fads?
    (vi) Does he suck or swallow inedible objects?

(*c*) *Washing*

    (i) Can he wash and dry his own hands, or his hands and face? Can he bath himself with or without help?
    (ii) Is he aware when his hands or face are dirty?

(*d*) *Dressing*

    (i) Can the child put on any of his garments by himself? Can he do up buttons and laces?
    (ii) Can he remove any of his garments? Can he undo buttons or laces?

064517

(iii) Can he brush and comb his own hair?
(iv) Can he brush his own teeth?
(v) Is he concerned if his clothes are dirty or untidy?

(*e*) *Continence*

(i) What stage has he reached in his toilet training in the daytime?
(ii) Is he clean and dry at night?

(*f*) *Independence*

(i) Can the child get objects that he wants for himself? Does he look for things that are hidden? Does he climb on a chair to reach things? Does he undo door handles and locks?
(ii) Is he aware of any dangers, e.g. from hot things, sharp things? Is he aware of the danger of heights or of deep water? Is he aware that traffic is dangerous? Does he know how to cross a road safely?
(iii) How much does he have to be supervised? Could he be allowed to go into another room alone; in the garden alone; in the street outside the house; around the local neighbourhood; or further afield? Could he travel on public transport alone?

XI. Sleep

(i) Does the child usually stay awake till very late at night or wake up very early in the morning? (Note usual times of going to sleep and waking.)
(ii) Is his sleep usually disturbed? Does he scream, or demand attention in other ways when he wakes in the night?

XII. Achievements in school work

(*a*) *General aspects*

(i) Length of attention span for different types of task.
(ii) Motivation for different types of tasks.

(b) *Specific skills*

N.B. In each case the child's ability to understand as well as to execute the tasks should be assessed.

   (i) Pre-reading skills, including ability to recognize objects in pictures.
  (ii) Reading.
 (iii) Writing.
 (iv) Number work; money; measurement.
  (v) Telling the time; days of the week; months of the year; giving the date.
 (vi) Drawing; painting; modelling.
(vii) Is the child able to cope with any school subjects beyond the basic skills, e.g. geography, biology, etc.?

XIII. Domestic and practical skills

   (i) Does the child help with laying and clearing the table; tidying up; cleaning; washing up; washing clothes, etc.? Can he use domestic equipment such as a vacuum cleaner? Does he help with shopping?
  (ii) Can he help with any aspect of preparing and cooking food?
 (iii) Can he knit or sew?
 (iv) Can he do woodwork?
  (v) Can he do any other craft work?

XIV. Other problems

Any abnormalities not covered in the other sections.

XV. The child's own personality

However handicapped a child is, he has his own personality which affects the way he reacts to his impairments of function. Autistic children are no exception. Despite all their problems it is possible to see that, for example, some are basically tough and outgoing, others are shy and timid, some are confident while others are anxious.

Careful consideration of this aspect is important because it should guide the way in which the techniques of teaching are applied.

Practical applications of the observations

Describing a child's behaviour by using the above scheme does not provide any overall assessment such as a developmental level or an intelligence quotient. All it can do is to give a standardized approach to defining a child's specific impairments, social handicaps, behaviour problems and any compensating skills as an essential part of a general medical and psychological assessment. It can, however, be of considerable assistance in the differential diagnosis. Children with the behaviour pattern characteristic of Kanner's autistic syndrome, as given in Chapter 1, can be identified. If a child has severe problems in comprehending and using speech but has the ability to communicate his needs by gesture and mime then the possibility of deafness or a specific developmental receptive speech delay should be investigated with special care. If a child does not talk but appears to have good comprehension of speech, can use non-spoken communication and has some imaginative play, then a developmental expressive speech delay should be suspected. Sometimes a child reveals practical and even academic skills in the familiar situation of home or classroom even though he has performed badly on standard intelligence tests. This finding indicates the need for further psychological investigations with particular attention to motivating the child to perform as well as he can.

When the assessment is completed it will be possible to see which problems stand out as most urgent. The results of the first observations should not be taken as the final indication of the child's abilities but should be used as the starting point for a programme of teaching skills and management of behavioural abnormalities. The full assessment, or else the parts relevant to the individual child, can be repeated at intervals in order to evaluate progress and the success or failure of the teaching techniques that are being used.

CHAPTER 3

ASSESSMENT: THE ROLE OF THE PSYCHOLOGIST

JUDITH GOULD

As emphasized in Chapter 2, full assessment of any handicapped child involves contributions from all the relevant professional workers, who should, ideally, work in collaboration with one another. This chapter will give a brief account of some of the methods used by psychologists and their advantages and limitations, since, of all the workers involved, apart from the teacher herself, the psychologist's findings have the most direct and immediate relevance to teaching. The psychologist's role in assessment is the examination of all kinds of mental functions, including cognitive, linguistic, perceptual, motor and social skills, by using special tests. An important part of this process is the estimation of the level of development any individual child has reached in each of these functions as compared with that expected in normal children.

General Problems in Using Psychological Tests

The majority of tests are based upon the assumption that it is possible to devise artificial situations easy to apply in the testing room which are models of situations met in real life. If this can be done there are obvious advantages to be gained. Observation of children in their daily life is extremely time consuming and difficult to arrange. It may easily happen with a handicapped child that his natural environment rarely or never presents him with tasks in which he can succeed, thus giving an impression of a greater degree of impairment than is actually the case. Behaviour problems exacerbated by his everyday environment may also reduce a child's level of performance. Special tests can be used to look at specific aspects of a child's functioning, the details of which may be impossible to disentangle from clinical observations alone. Finally, tests can be standardized and given in the same way each time, allowing comparisons between different children, whereas the natural environment is anything but standard.

Given these advantages, it is not surprising that psychologists have devised "laboratory" tests, the best of which have been developed with great care and which have been proved to be extremely helpful when used for the purpose for which they were designed. On the other hand, the usefulness and relevance of psychological tests should not be accepted uncritically. Sometimes the artificial laboratory situations are based on extremely naive views of the real-life function that they represent. Such tests, partly because they have been refined to examine one or a few areas of function only, do leave out many aspects of human behaviour, such as motivation and determination, which are important for success in life or in compensating for handicaps.

One of the most important applications of psychological testing is the estimation of general ability and potential for learning by the use of intelligence tests. These tests are standardized on large groups of normal children covering the whole age range for which the test is devised. It is therefore possible to compare a child's score with those obtained for each age group in the standard sample and to assign an approximate "mental age" (M.A.) on the basis of this comparison. The significance of a mental age obviously varies with the child's chronological age (C.A.) so the scores are often transformed into an "intelligence quotient" (I.Q.). This is a way of relating one child's score to the range of scores expected from all the children in his age group. If the mean IQ is 100, then a child with an IQ of 90 is performing less well than the average for his age while one with an IQ of 110 is performing better than the average. The way the IQ is calculated varies with different tests.

There are other ways of expressing a child's performance as compared with those of other children of his age, in addition to the

IQ. The only one that will be mentioned here, because it is used in one of the tests to be described below, is the percentile score. This represents the percentage of people in the standardization sample who fall below the score obtained by the individual being tested. If someone has a percentile score of 60, then he did better than 60 per cent of the subjects on whom the test was standardized. The higher the score the better the performance.

Some special problems arise in the use of tests for measuring intelligence. One of the most important of these is the assumption that it is possible to use one test, or a collection of tests (known as a test battery), in order to produce a single score which gives useful information concerning an individual's general intellectual abilities. This is rather like trying to judge the quality of a stew by sampling some of the individual ingredients, although the essence of the dish is in their combination. There is some justification for this assumption. If (for example) large groups of children without known handicaps affecting intellectual function are tested, using test batteries that have been carefully worked out and standardized, then it can be seen that most of the high scorers are those who do well in class and in examinations, while the low scorers tend to be the poor achievers. When the results of individuals are looked at, however, it is found that while most score fairly evenly on all the sub-tests some people have quite marked discrepancies between one type of skill and another. In this situation an average score means that some information about the way the individual functions is obscured.

When working with handicapped children or adults, the difficulties of assigning an average score become very obvious. Skills in one area are not matched by skills in another, so the calculation of a single intelligence quotient or mental age has limited value. The scores cannot be used to compare children with different handicaps. An autistic child with an IQ of 50 will present a completely different picture from a child with Down's syndrome with the same IQ (Wing, 1969). Psychologists are now well aware of these problems but, in the past, some confusion has arisen, especially in the field of childhood autism. Kanner's incorrect assumption that the existence of one or a few special skills in an autistic child inevitably meant that the child had all-round good cognitive potential was mentioned in Chapter 2.

A child's intelligence quotient measured at one age does not necessarily remain the same throughout his life. Development may speed up or slow down at any stage, thus changing the IQ as compared with previous tests. The tests themselves are imperfect instruments because often the sub-tests designed for different age ranges call for different types of skills, and may give very different results as a handicapped child grows older. Autistic children are at a special disadvantage because tests for younger age groups tend to emphasize motor skills, but most of those for older children depend much more on the ability to use language. In general, for any child, the younger he is the less easy it is to predict his future scores from a current test. Under 5 years old, intelligence test scores are very poor predictors indeed.

Scores obtained for the same person on different tests or test batteries are likely to be different, especially for people with handicaps. Even with very skilful testing, using reliable tests, a person may score differently when given the same test on two occasions for a variety of reasons, such as health, mood, or level of alertness, which are difficult to control.

Despite all these problems, psychological tests have proved their value in medical and educational practice and research. A balanced view which takes into account both the limitations and the advantages of the tests is necessary if they are to be a useful part of the assessment process. A most helpful discussion of the value of cognitive assessment in young children with language delay (including autistic children) has been written by Berger and Yule (1972).

Testing Autistic Children

Psychological testing, using appropriate methods, is important in assessing autistic children. Some of the standardized batteries of tests for measuring intelligence, to be mentioned below, are useful in providing an overall view of the impairments and skills of an autistic child. Autistic behaviour may occur in association with any level of intelligence. Behaviour disturbances or lack of appropriate teaching may make a child appear very retarded on clinical observation but skilful testing may elicit unsuspected abilities.

Specialized tests, for example of language function, should be used to explore specific problems which clinical observations suggest may be an important part of the picture.

This combination of general and special assessment can help to decide appropriate educational placement and provide information for planning a programme of teaching (see Chapters 5 and 6) and behaviour modification (see Chapter 4). It can be most helpful for the psychologist and teacher to collaborate in a continuing re-evaluation of each child's progress. If problems found in teaching are discussed and explored by classroom observations and specially devised tests, it may be possible to find solutions more quickly than by trial and error.

Psychological tests can be used to estimate the amount of progress an autistic child is likely to make. The children's scores on tests which do not depend on language correlate well with eventual prognosis (Rutter and Lockyer, 1967; Rutter, Greenfeld and Lockyer, 1967; De Myer *et al.*, 1973). This is an interesting finding and one which provides evidence for the relevance of psychological testing in this field, even though autistic children are particularly difficult to test. It is especially important to obtain a psychological assessment on a child whose disturbed behaviour gives the impression of severe retardation.

A major cause of the difficulty in applying most of the possible tests to autistic children is that they have been devised and standardized on children who are within the normal range of intelligence and who have no known handicaps. It is inappropriate to apply them uncritically to children, such as those who are autistic or severely mentally retarded, whose development in many ways differs markedly from the normal.

Autistic children and those with similar handicaps affecting comprehension of language are the most extreme example of a group who have large discrepancies between different types of skills. In particular, they have special problems in comprehending and using language and in handling symbols, which vary greatly in severity between different children, but which are always present to some degree. Many psychological tests depend on verbal explanation of the task to be done or require the child to have some ability to manipulate symbols and concepts internally. Autistic children, even those with good non-language dependent skills may fail to perform a task which they are capable of doing because they cannot grasp what is required of them. A typical story is that of autistic twins who did not co-operate at all in a psychological test when asked to make a tower of blocks. About half an hour later, outside the test room, the psychologist found the twins absorbed in building a tower of empty milk bottles to an astonishing height, a much harder task than piling up little wooden cubes.

In such a situation it is tempting to suggest that the child is wilfully refusing to co-operate, but, if some way can be found of "making the penny drop" then he usually does the task to the best of his ability.

Often the only way in which an autistic child's true level of performance on non-language dependent skills can be measured is to use the operant techniques of concrete demonstration, prompting and rewarding as a preliminary to testing. If a test involves a series of items graded in severity but all utilizing the same kind of operation (e.g. Raven's matrices, see page 41) then the first one or two items can be used for training. For many tests, this procedure is completely contrary to the rules which often specify a set of standard instructions (given verbally, non-verbally or both) which must be used without any deviation. These rules are essential for most research and clinical work, but there are good reasons for bending them when exploring the specific impairments and skills of autistic children and those with related conditions. The aim in this case is not to compare the results with those obtained in normal children, but to discover what the child can and cannot do and what factors help him to perform most effectively. Discovering how to help the child grasp what is required of him in itself gives valuable information concerning the limitations of his comprehension of language and the ways in which he can be motivated to perform.

Autistic children are often especially sensitive to failure. If they realize that they have performed incorrectly they may withdraw or have a violent temper tantrum. Either way, co-operation is lost and testing becomes impossible for the time being. It is always useful for the psychologist to discuss a child with the teacher before testing so that, among other things, he can learn if the child has this problem and also the kinds of things which the child sees as rewarding and those which he dislikes.

Because autistic children cannot be tested satisfactorily simply by following the routine procedures, it is clear that considerable experience in the field is essential before a psychologist can produce reliable and useful results. Sympathetic understanding of the children's handicaps, familiarity with the principles and practice of learning theory and a firm and confident approach are necessary for success. Testing by inexperienced people has given rise to the common belief that results with autistic children are completely unreliable and vary wildly from one occasion to another. The truth is that psychological tests, in the hands of a skilful and experienced psychologist, are reliable and helpful, but may be worse than useless if given by a novice in the field of autism.

Descriptions of Some Tests

A great number of psychological tests for a wide variety of different purposes are available (Anastasi, 1968). Only a few which are often used with autistic children and other children with severe language problems will be mentioned here, in order to give some idea of the types of tasks set in psychological testing, their purpose, and any special problems that may be found when using them with children of this kind.[1]

1. Tests of intellectual development

(a) The Merrill–Palmer Scale of Mental Tests

The Merrill–Palmer Scales can be used with children whose mental ages are between 18 months and 71 months. It consists of a collection of sub-tests which are arranged in increasing order of

---

[1]Examples of test items given here are analogous to but not the same as those used in actual tests.

difficulty. Some of them require varying levels of understanding and use of speech while others are tests of performance which can be demonstrated without using words or else can be taught by operant conditioning techniques as mentioned previously. The tests requiring language include, for example, simple questions such as "What does the birdie say?", "What is your name?", for the younger children and for the older ones more difficult questions such as "What hops along?", "What writes?". The performance tests include fitting pegs in peg boards, assembling picture puzzles and matching shapes which requires logical reasoning and therefore can be done even by children who do not have any system of symbols for communication.

This test battery is especially useful with the younger autistic child, or the older child with a mental age within the range for which the scale was designed. The majority of the items are of the "performance" kind. It is constructed in such a way that the tester can make allowances for the items which are omitted or which the child refuses to try so that he is given full credit for those which he does complete. This is a great advantage when testing children who are unable to do any of the verbal items, or with disturbed children whose attention can be held only long enough to complete a few of the sub-tests. The test materials are interesting even to the most withdrawn or difficult child. All the items are packed in different, brightly coloured boxes of varying sizes and since there is no definite order of presentation the child can choose what he wants to do next.

The Merrill–Palmer Scale, among other items, contains the test known as the Seguin form board, consisting of a wooden board with different shaped holes into which wooden pieces can be fitted. It is a particular favourite with many autistic children who are often able to complete this with speed and skill even though their abilities in other areas may be at a much lower level. One child tested by the author who had no spoken and very limited comprehension of language inserted the pieces into the Seguin board correctly first time and then, on the second trial, wanted to restack the pieces herself in front of the board so that she could insert them in their holes again as quickly and efficiently as possible.

The main disadvantage of the Merrill–Palmer Scale is that the limited age range makes it unsuitable for use with older autistic children who have good non-verbal skills. Another disadvantage is that the scoring depends on speed as well as accuracy of performance. Some autistic children are slowed up because of their rituals; for example, one child insisted upon licking, smelling and tapping twice upon each piece of equipment before placing it correctly. Another child lost time because of the obsessional accuracy with which he arranged each piece in the performance tasks. These problems are, however, outweighed by the usefulness of the scale for the younger and also for the severely retarded autistic children.

The scale gives a mental age, but the calculation of an IQ is not appropriate for statistical reasons related to the design of the test.

(b) *The Wechsler Tests*

The Wechsler Tests include the Wechsler Pre-school and Primary Scale of Intelligence (WPPSI) for the age range 4 to $6\frac{1}{2}$ years and the Wechsler Intelligence Scale for Children (WISC) for the age range 5 to 15 years 11 months. (There is also a Wechsler Scale for Adults which will not be discussed here.) The original Wechsler Tests were developed in America but the WPPSI has now been standardized on a British sample of children and various modifications have been made (Yule *et al.*, 1969).

Both the WPPSI and the WISC have the same basic design. They consist of ten sub-tests each of which contains items of the same type but arranged in order of increasing difficulty. The ten sub-tests fall into two groups of five, one group containing the "verbal" items and the other the "performance" items.

Taking the WISC for illustration, the verbal items consist of questions to elicit general knowledge; comprehension of the appropriate action to be taken in various situations (e.g. "What would you do if you tore your coat?"); explaining the similarities between pairs of words (e.g. pen and pencil); definitions of words; and arithmetical problems. The "performance" items are picture completion (pointing out the item that is missing from an otherwise complete picture);

arranging pictures in the order which tells a logical story; copying various arrangements of coloured blocks; arranging the pieces of a picture that has been cut up, to form the complete picture again; and coding (i.e. learning to use one shape to represent another shape or a shape to represent a number).

The problem in using the Wechsler Tests with autistic children and others with severe language problems is that the distinction between the verbal and the so-called performance items is somewhat dubious. In particular, the picture completion, picture arrangement and the coding tests do not ask for a spoken response but the ability to reason logically in words or in some other system of symbols whether in silent thought or out loud is essential for their completion. Rutter (1968) has shown that autistic children do poorly on these sub-tests. One autistic girl, who had a very large vocabulary, when presented with the picture arrangement task, placed the cards in random order. When asked to explain, she listed the contents of each picture but did not link them together at all. On the other hand some autistic children do well on copying designs with coloured blocks and assembling cut-up pictures. The high correlation between verbal and performance scales found when testing large groups of non-handicapped people underlines the fact that there is a large overlap between the two. An autistic child may therefore obtain very different scores when given the truly non-verbal items of the Merrill–Palmer Scale and the performance items on the WPPSI.

The Wechsler scales give a verbal IQ, a performance IQ and an overall "full scale" IQ score.

(c) The Stanford–Binet Intelligence Scale

A number of modifications of this scale exists. One which is commonly used is known as the Form L-M. It covers the age range from 2 years up to "superior adult" level and is frequently used by school medical officers when assessing children for special education. It is, however, particularly unsuitable for children with autism or with other kinds of language problems because so many of the items involve verbal ability (Berger and Yule, 1972).

The scale consists of a collection of many different sub-tests grouped according to different age ranges. Those for the 2 to $2\frac{1}{2}$ year olds include a simple form board, picture vocabulary and identifying objects by name. Children aged 8 to 9 years are tested on, for example, their memory for stories, detection of verbal absurdities and their ability to explain the similarities and differences between objects such as a penknife and scissors. The tests for the older age groups are even more dependent upon vocabulary and abstract reasoning. No one who is familiar with autistic children will be surprised to learn that they tend to score lower on this scale than on the Merrill–Palmer. The Stanford–Binet could perhaps be of some use in exploring the subtle handicaps in the use of abstract reasoning in an older child with good performance in some fields who is suspected of being mildly autistic. There is no justification for its use in deciding appropriate school placement for the young autistic child since it would give a most inadequate picture of those skills which he may possess.

The Stanford–Binet Scale allows the calculation of one overall IQ score.

(d) Raven's Progressive Matrices

The standard form of the progressive matrices consists of sixty designs. Each design has one piece missing and the appropriate piece to complete the design has to be chosen from a number of alternatives. The designs are arranged in five groups of twelve. Within each group the designs gradually increase in difficulty but the principle remains the same throughout. The test can be used for children of 8 years upwards and for adults. There is also a version using coloured patterns which is described as suitable for normal children aged from 5 to 11 years, old people, those who for reasons of background or disability cannot understand or speak English and for mentally retarded children and adults.

The test does not call for any verbal responses and it is supposed to test reasoning skills not involving speech. It examines such abilities as visual discrimination and in the later, more difficult, groups of designs, the capacity to see analogies and other logical relationships. There is no time limit for its performance.

Some autistic children have excellent visuo-spatial skills and, providing they understand what is required of them, are able to do the coloured matrices and, possibly, some of the items of the standard form. In these cases the test is useful in showing the kinds of logical operations available to the child, which could be utilized for teaching. Children who have visual perceptual problems in addition to autism will have difficulty in performing this test whatever their ability with logical reasoning.

There is a board form of the coloured matrices in which the pieces can be fitted into the design like an inset puzzle. This could be much more easily demonstrated to children with language problems than the usual book form where the subject has to point to or mark the missing piece, but the board form is not available commercially. The score obtained on this test is expressed as a percentile.

(e) The Columbia Mental Maturity Scale

This scale with age range 3 years to 10 years was developed primarily for use with cerebral palsied children, and consists of a set of cards each bearing a series of drawings in bright colours or a series of written words. The task is to choose the one item in each set which does not fit. The early ones are simple; for example, a series consisting of two red circles and a yellow square in which the odd one out is distinguished both by colour and shape. The later ones are much more difficult; for example a series of pictures of things in motion only one of which is animate. Some of the series are printed words; for example "car, bus, train, river".

The earlier, simpler series can be used for training in order to ensure that the child grasps the idea of the task. The problems in using the scale with autistic children arise from the inclusion of written series as well as pictorial ones and the combination of increasing visual complexity together with increasing complexity of concepts many of which require logical reasoning to resolve. Because of this mixture of dimensions of difficulty the hierarchy of difficulty laid down in the test is not appropriate for autistic children who may be able to do some of the supposedly harder, later items but miss out on the earlier ones.

The usefulness of the scale as applied to autistic children lies in the clues it can give to the types of concepts an individual child is able to handle and those which he cannot grasp.

A mental age and an IQ can be calculated from the scores.

(*f*) *The Leiter International Performance Scale*

The Leiter Scale was developed for use with deaf children. The materials consist of a series of picture cards and sets of small wooden cubes each with a picture on one face. The picture cards are displayed in turn in a frame. The child has to match the pictures on the blocks with those on the cards and then place the blocks in the holes provided in the frame, adjacent to the appropriate picture on the card. The instructions are given entirely by demonstration and do not require any words at all. The items cover the age range 2 to 18 years.

The earlier items include matching on colour, shape, design and number. Some depend on matching by analogy. Later items in the scale involve the ability to visualize in three dimensions.

The absence of verbal instructions makes this test very suitable for autistic children. The more able ones enjoy doing the earlier items which are completely non-language dependent. As with the Columbia Scale it is interesting to see which concepts are intact and which are not. One child did all the items up to the 7-year level with accuracy and speed except for one which required her to match pictures of people on the basis of age. The same child, when matching articles of clothing to appropriate parts of the body, revealed her tendency to expressive dysphasia and perseveration by saying "hand-hat" when putting the glove by the hand and "foot-glove" when placing the shoe by the foot.

The scale gives a mental age and an IQ.

2. Tests of social development

A child's ability in self-care skills and the way he interacts with other people can develop at a different rate from his intellectual skills, especially if he has some handicapping condition. Just as tests of intelligence assign a mental age so it is possible to give a child a social age by measuring his practical and social achievements and comparing them with a sample population of normal children.

(a) *The Vineland Social Maturity Scale*

This widely used scale assesses the child's ability to look after his own practical needs. It covers eight different areas. These are general self-help, eating, dressing, locomotion, occupation, communication, self-direction and socialization. The person who knows the child best is interviewed in order to elicit the information necessary for making a rating on each particular item. There is no set list of questions to be asked, but the booklet gives, for each item, a series of examples of behaviour that should be present in order to say that the skill has been achieved. The experienced interviewer directs his questioning in order to obtain relevant examples of the child's everyday behaviour. For example, when trying to rate a child on the item "follows simple instructions" he will ask what happens when the child is called; how does he respond if sent to a particular place; is he able to point to objects in pictures when they are named; can he perform baby games when asked to do so. If these examples are not relevant to the lifestyle of the family concerned he will use equivalent but more appropriate examples. The age range covered is from under one month to over 25 years.

Some autistic children may score lower on this scale than on truly non-language dependent intelligence tests because many of the items depend on the comprehension and use of language both for social communication and for thinking and planning ahead. It is therefore more informative to look at the pattern of scores for the individual autistic child than at his overall social age, which can be calculated from the child's total score on the scale.

Although not ideal, the Vineland Scale can give some clue as to the level of development of an autistic child who is functioning as very severely retarded and who appears to be unable to cope with any of the more formal tests, even with preliminary training.

(b) The Gunzberg Progress Assessment Chart

This, as its author states, is *not* a test but a chart for recording the stages reached by individuals in self-help skills (eating, mobility, toilet training, washing and dressing) communication, socialization and occupation. The items under each heading can be rated as present or absent and marked on the chart accordingly. This gives a profile of skills and deficiencies in a readily assimilated pictorial form. Later assessments can be compared with earlier ones and progress, or lack of it, can be easily seen.

This chart was designed specifically for mentally retarded children and adults of all ages. It is therefore sometimes applied to autistic children attending schools or hospitals for those who are mentally retarded. It is a useful summary, but some of the items, especially those in the section on communication, are difficult to rate in autistic children. The biggest deficiency of the chart in its use with these children is the absence of any rating of the behavioural abnormalities which are of such importance in planning treatment and rating progress.

3. Tests of language development

Testing the level of language development and looking for language abnormalities is a crucial part of the psychological assessment of autistic children. Three such tests which are often used with autistic children will be described here.

(a) The Peabody Picture Vocabulary Test

This test is presented in the form of a booklet. Each page has four pictures. The tester says a word and the child has to point to the corresponding picture. The number of correct responses is counted and the child is also rated for rapport, speed of response, verbalization, attention span, attentiveness, guessing and for pauses before responding. It should be noted that the child has only four different pictures from which to choose so if he guesses he has a one-in-four chance of being correct. The test covers the age range 2 years 6 months to 18 years. There are alternative forms so that the test can be repeated at a later date without very much effect due to practice.

The original Peabody Test was standardized on American children and many of the words do not have the same frequency in an English vocabulary. An English version has been produced consisting of two tests, one for the age range 5 years to 8 years 11 months and one for 7 years to 11 years 11 months. There is also a pre-school supplement for the age range 3 years to 4 years 11 months.

This test measures the size of the vocabulary of words understood by the child and not his spoken vocabulary or his ability to use language. In normal children language skills and vocabulary size usually develop together so that the Peabody score does give some idea of general language skills. This is not true of autistic children, some of whom may have extensive vocabularies but very limited ability to use the rules of grammar or to use language for thinking and planning. The Peabody Test therefore has only a limited place in assessing autistic children.

The scores can be used to calculate mental age and IQ.

(b) The Reynell Developmental Language Scale

These scales have been developed with English children and cover the age range 5 months to 6 years 1 month. The test materials consist of a set of miniature objects including small dolls, furniture, clothing, domestic and farmyard animals, plus a set of five pictures taken from the Ladybird book series illustrating the everyday activities of a family.

The scales attempt to measure two fundamental aspects of language; firstly, the process of interpreting what is heard (receptive language) and, secondly, the ability to express ideas in words (expressive language). These are often referred to as "central" processes, meaning that they depend on the higher levels of brain activity and are *not* simply a question of hearing and speaking words.

The verbal comprehension scale (version "A") is divided into nine sections, which follow the normal pattern of development of understanding of language. The earliest section concerns the pre-verbal stage in which the child is not yet using verbal labelling but understands some sounds that have emotional significance for him; for example, the child is rated on whether or not he looks at a familiar object or person when he hears the name. In later sections the child is asked to point to or arrange the toys in response to instructions; for example, "Which dog has the lead on?" "Show me how the boy jumps over the gate." In the last section the child has to understand a situation and describe or demonstrate the consequences; for example, the boy doll is placed on a chair in front of the table and the tester says, "This little boy has dropped his cup. What must he do?" The sections demand progressively more ability to abstract and to understand sequences.

Reynell has developed a second comprehension scale "B". This was designed for physically handicapped children and requires a minimum of response from the child. It follows the same developmental stages as Scale A but it is slightly easier at the upper end of the test. Separate norms are provided for this scale.

The expressive scale is divided into three sections; these are language structure, vocabulary, and content.

The language structure section covers the development of vocalization from the earliest stage of "vocalization other than crying", up to the use of complex sentences, omitting no words and with the words in the correct order. This is rated from the child's vocalization during the test.

The simplest part of the vocabulary section requires the child to name various miniature objects. The next stage is naming objects or activities in pictures. The hardest task is defining a series of words, including nouns, verbs and one adjective. These are given orally, without any visual aids—for example "What is an orange?". The child is not given any score if he demonstrates by gesture instead of using words as some children with Dowen's syndrome (mongolism) may do.

The "content" section, according to Reynell, "assesses the more creative use of language". In order to obtain a high score the child must be able to verbalize connected thoughts. The five pictures from the Ladybird book series are shown one by one to the child and he is asked to describe what he sees. The score depends on the adequacy and complexity of the description. This is probably the hardest part of the whole test to score since there are obviously no standard responses, the children being free to say what they like.

One problem is that some children do not realize what is required in this section. The instruction is simply, "Tell me about this picture". If there is no response or if the child says very little, one prompt is allowed on the first picture only. This must be a neutral remark such as "Is there anything else?". No other help may be given and no preliminary demonstration by example is allowed. Very verbal children have no difficulty but a shy, withdrawn child may say little, whereas some prompting would bring out much more. It should also be remembered that some handicapped children, especially those brought up or in institutions or even those living in towns, may not know the names of farmyard animals through lack of opportunity. They would therefore be unfairly penalized on some items.

The Reynell Scales are interesting ones to use with autistic children. Some of them are able to name a wide range of objects but have no ability at all to link ideas together. With the type of autistic child who has enough language to attempt to perform some of the tasks it is of particular interest to note the nature of the mistakes made, in addition to the usual scoring. Bartak (personal communication) has found that autistic children have most difficulty in understanding those parts of speech which relate one object or action to another and which change in meaning depending on the situation. They therefore make mistakes with, for example, prepositions and pronouns, which affects their performance on the scales.

While most autistic children have marked problems with grammatical structures a few are able to produce grammatically correct speech by the time of later childhood. These children may be able to perform well on the Reynell Scales. The tests do not show up the stilted, rather pedantic, speech found in such children, nor do they demonstrate the limited scope and stereotyped nature of their language.

The Reynell Scales give a language age for comprehension and another for expression.

(c) *The Illinois Test of Psycholinguistic Abilities*

The age range covered by this test is from 2 years 3 months to 9 years 3 months. It has been standardized on American children so some of the items are unfamiliar to children in the United Kingdom. The material consists of picture cards and a few miniature objects. The idea behind the test is that language ability can be broken down into different skills, each of which can be tested separately. Six of the sub-tests are intended to examine the development of meaningful language. The first two deal with "decoding" which is the understanding of a word or a picture, the second two with "association", or the ability to grasp the relationship between words or pictures, and the last two with "encoding" or the process of expressing ideas in words or gestures. For each of these three pairs of sub-tests, one involves hearing words and giving a vocal response (auditory-vocal) while the other involves seeing a picture and giving a motor response (visual-motor). To give some examples, the auditory decoding test consists of a series of questions such as "Do birds fly?" which the child has to answer "Yes" or "No". In the vocal encoding tests the child is asked to describe a simple object such as a piece of chalk.

For the motor encoding test, the child has to use miming to demonstrate the use of various objects. Initially there are real objects, e.g. a pencil and then the objects are shown in pictures, e.g. a telescope, a piano, a screwdriver.

The remaining three sub-tests examine language functions which the authors of the test suggest are habitual or automatic rather than reasoned. One sub-test examines the ability to use grammatical rules, the second looks at immediate memory by asking the child to repeat a string of up to seven digits and the third concerns visual memory of the arrangement of a series of picture cards.

This way of breaking down language is arguable, but it can be useful in testing those autistic children who have sufficient language to be able to try to do the tests. Tubbs (1966) used the Illinois Test to compare children with childhood psychosis of early onset with normal children and with children who were severely retarded but without psychotic behaviour. She found that psychotic children were particularly poor in those tests requiring the expression of ideas in speech, or, even more markedly, in gesture. They were also handicapped in transforming material given in one form (e.g. visual) into another form (e.g. verbal).

The Illinois Test gives a language age for each sub-test and an overall language age can be calculated from the sub-test ages.

(d) Assessment of Language through Play Behaviour

Mary Sheridan has developed a technique for making observations of the play behaviour of young children aged from 12 months to 4 years, since this provides information on the acquisition of "inner language" (Sheridan, 1969).

The materials consist firstly of a series of common objects such as brush and comb, cup and spoon, and some commonly used toys; secondly of a set of miniature baby dolls, domestic animals, household objects and furniture, and a car, ship and plane.

The common objects can be used from 12 months of age onwards. The child's spontaneous reactions and manipulations of the objects are observed to see if he understands their purpose. The miniatures are used from about 21 months of age. They are presented one by one and the child's reactions, verbalizations or gesture and miming noted. Then his ability to understand instructions involving prepositions, to carry out a sequence of commands and to invent and describe make-believe situations is tested, using the miniatures.

The procedure cannot be used to derive any kind of score, but it is a good way of obtaining information about the development of the use of symbols. It was devised specifically for children with language problems. The child who, for example, does not speak because he has difficulty with expressive speech although he comprehends well will show through his play that he is developing symbolic play and inner language. The young classically autistic child on the other hand will manipulate the miniatures in a way which shows that he has little or no comprehension of what they represent, and he will certainly not show any evidence of imaginative play.

4. Experimental methods of assessment

When discussing the above tests, it was emphasized that a number of them were too language dependent to give a fair picture of an autistic child's skills. While this is true, it is necessary to preserve a sense of proportion on this point. Intelligence tests almost always have a marked bias towards testing skills needing language (that is the use of some system of symbols) because this is an essential part of intellectual development and is absolutely vital for an independent life as an adult. The autistic child's failure on most intelligence tests is a fair comment on the severity of his handicaps which are almost always life-long. It is nevertheless legitimate to look for tests which can show the child's special skills so that he can be helped to make the best use of these to compensate as much as possible for his deficiencies in understanding and using any system of communication.

The tests described have a place in assessing autistic children but none of them was designed with the peculiar needs of this group in mind. Some recent research work in the field of psychology includes some tests which were devised to examine specific problems in autistic children. Hermelin, O'Connor, Frith and their colleagues (Hermelin and O'Connor, 1970; Frith, 1971; Hermelin, 1975) have contributed a great deal to this field. They have shown, among many other findings, that autistic children have particular problems in handling symbols, especially in organizing material in a logical sequence in time. The children tend to impose very simple, stereotyped, repetitive patterns on their sensory input instead of appreciating the complex relationship between one object or event and another. Their ability to memorize, on the other hand, is often very good, but they remember a nonsensical sequence just as easily as a logical one, unlike normal children who remember meaningful material better than a sequence without connecting links.

Churchill (1972) used an ingenious method of testing autistic children involving an artificial "language" containing 3 nouns, 3 adjectives and 3 verbs which were expressed in visual shapes, spoken words and gestured signs. The children were systematically taught this language and then their ability to use it was tested. They showed the expected problems in comprehension and sequencing and in handling the syntax and structure of language. The most interesting finding, however, was that while there were some general problems common to the group, each individual child showed his own pattern of language difficulties which was reliable on re-testing. It is easy to see how such a detailed assessment of individual children could provide a teacher with information she could use to plan her teaching programme. Such inventiveness and willingness to experiment outside the conventional limits of standard tests is to be welcomed in clinical and educational work with autistic children as well as in research.

One field which requires further exploration is the social naivety which is such a handicap even to the more able autistic child and which is painfully obvious in the adult. If this could be analysed to identify the specific problems contributing to the typical social behaviour pattern it might be possible to devise training methods to compensate for the handicap.

It would also be helpful if satisfactory tests of perception could be designed which were applicable to autistic children. No one knows how these children experience the world. Their behaviour in early childhood suggests that they may have many difficulties in organizing sensory input at the central level. At the moment it is not possible to say if this is an integral part of their problem in using symbols, or whether this is an additional handicap exacerbating the former but different in nature. If these problems could be measured and analysed we should be nearer to understanding the nature of childhood autism.

In applying tests to an autistic child it is of more value to give details of his performance on the different parts of the test, the way he approached the tasks, his behaviour during the test and his response to the examiner, than it is to give a single numerical score. The tests are to be used as a basis for constructive action to help the child, not as a label or a convenient excuse to stop trying to help him any more.

CHAPTER 4

MANAGEMENT OF BEHAVIOUR PROBLEMS

ROSEMARY HEMSLEY and PATRICIA HOWLIN

I. Principles and Approaches of Treatment

Autistic children present many problems of management and education in the classroom. The severity and nature of these problems will vary very much from child to child and consequently the methods used to deal with behaviour problems must vary accordingly. In order to determine the most effective programme of management for any one child the teacher needs to use his own observations of that child to decide first of all what the main problems are and the circumstances in which they occur.

The application of an individual treatment approach to the problems shown by autistic children involves an analysis of these problems in a specific way. In the following five sections we consider the factors which need to be taken into account in the case of each child.

1. Identification of the problem

When describing the child's problems the teacher should be as precise as possible, and the behaviours which he wishes to change should be set out in concise terms so that they may be worked on directly. Thus, a child who is "aggressive" in the classroom might show a number of distinct behaviours, for example:

(a) Taking other children's toys.
(b) Lashing out at other children when made to do something he does not like.

(c) Hitting children and pulling their hair when not occupied in any other activity.

Such behaviours taken together add up to an aggressive and disruptive child but by identifying and treating the problems individually the task of dealing with them becomes much more manageable.

The autistic child will, of course, be lacking in many normal skills as well as showing undesirable behaviours, and these too should be described in specific rather than general terms. For example a child who is "not able to talk" might pose problems of:

(a) Not being able to understand instructions,
(b) Not being able to name objects,
(c) Not being able to indicate his needs and wishes,

and each of these would be a major area in which to begin work. Thus it is important at the outset to formulate a clear idea of the aims which are to be achieved.

2. Tailoring the treatment to the individual child

Once the teacher has identified a problem behaviour in precise terms he then needs to consider how the teaching situation as a whole affects the child's behaviour. It is essential to view the problem behaviour in terms of what happens before it, what happens afterwards and also whether there are any long-standing factors which influence it.

(a) Precipitants of the behaviour

If the teacher looks carefully at the situation in which the difficulty arises he will often find that many problem behaviours, such as tantrums, refusal to co-operate or indulgence in rituals, are directly triggered off by particular events. It is therefore necessary to change the event which precedes the undesirable behaviour in order to reduce the likelihood of its recurrence. For example, in some cases it may be necessary to remove a child's treasured object if he is to be taught to use other materials appropriately. If this invariably results in a tantrum in a particular child it would be preferable to attack the problem by gradually reducing the child's dependence on the object rather than by taking it away from him abruptly and risking disruption to the whole class.

Similarly many outbursts of temper or destructive behaviour may be caused by the child's inability to make his needs and wishes known. Teaching the child to use simple words or gestures to indicate his wants frequently results in a very rapid decline in disruptive behaviours and is often far more effective than attempting to work directly on the tantrums themselves.

(b) Maintaining behaviours

Just as behaviours can be precipitated by particular circumstances they can also be prolonged by events which immediately *follow* the child's behaviour. Many outbursts of screaming or temper tantrums, however they were initiated, can be prolonged or even aggravated by attention from an adult or other children. If all attention is withdrawn from the child following each outburst the frequency and severity of such behaviours will diminish.

In a similar way it is possible to build up the number of skills and the amount of time the child spends involved in constructive activities by altering the events which follow these behaviours. If, for example, each time the child completes a simple jigsaw he is praised and given a hug or allowed to play with a favourite toy, the number of such puzzles he will complete will steadily increase. Conversely, if his efforts are not attended to and he is ignored while he is quiet and occupied, it is likely that he will soon stop working in this way. If a child who is attempting to use sounds to obtain a drink or toy is given the object he is asking for as soon as he makes an effort to speak, this is likely to increase his use of sounds on the next occasion. If, on the other hand, the adult is too busy to pay attention to his primitive efforts at communication and fails to recognize his needs, he is less likely to try to make an appropriate sound the next time he wants something, and will probably revert to screaming instead.

Autistic children, like any other children, need to be treated as individuals and it is essential that each child is closely observed by the teacher to see which events will strengthen and maintain desirable behaviours and skills, and to identify those which will lead to the reduction of undesirable behaviours. Once these events have been clearly identified it is then possible to use them to adapt the child's behaviour so that he learns skills more rapidly and shows fewer undesirable behaviours.

(c) Indirect factors influencing behaviour

It is also necessary for the teacher to be aware that other and less obvious aspects of the child's environment may influence his behaviour. The teacher may find that a child who usually responds well in the teaching situation may suddenly become irritable and lose interest if the teacher himself is tired or ill, or under additional strain. Similarly, the child can also be greatly influenced by factors in the home situation. A child who suddenly begins to show a great increase in tantrum behaviour may be affected by depression in his mother or by other problems at home. In such a case the most effective way to deal with the *child's* problem behaviour would be to help the mother in the first instance. It is also found that aggressive, destructive or ritualistic behaviours become far more frequent when the child is unoccupied and bored. In this case the obvious remedy is to provide more appropriate stimulation for the child in the classroom in order to minimize the occurrence of the undesirable behaviours.

3. The child's level of skills

When planning treatment and education for the autistic child it is necessary to assess accurately the level of skill each child possesses in many different areas of ability. The child's capacity for using and understanding language, his aptitude for non-verbal tasks, the level of his play behaviour, the manner in which he relates to other children as well as his ability in academic skills such as reading, writing and arithmetic, all need to be carefully recorded. In most cases merely observing the child's behaviour in the classroom for a few days will be enough to determine where the main problems lie as well as what the child's particular skills are. Work can then begin on major areas of deficit, particularly those such as a profound language handicap which prevent the child benefiting fully from the school situation, and on building up any special skills which the child already possesses.

Prior assessment of the child's deficits and capabilities ensures that teaching begins at an appropriate level for each individual child and avoids wasting time and energy in teaching the child tasks which are either much too easy or too difficult for him.

If, because a child is very withdrawn or unco-operative in the classroom there is any doubt about the true level of his skills, testing by a psychologist may be a useful adjunct to the teacher's own observations.

4. Structuring the teaching situation

The teaching environment should be organized so that specific skills can be actively encouraged and appropriate behaviours are more likely to occur. The teacher will already have observed which events seem to precipitate problem behaviours and by careful structuring of the classroom and materials used, many problems can be averted before they arise. The child's day should be organized so that short periods of formal work alternate with freer activities such as painting, playing with constructional toys such as "Lego" or looking at picture books. In this way each child in the class will receive individual adult attention at certain times of the day and can be directed to some extent during less organized periods.

The teaching materials need to be carefully selected for each individual child. Autistic children rarely possess abilities at the same overall level; some are advanced in social behaviour but poor in academic skills; others possess little language but have considerable aptitude for constructional tasks; still others may possess a single isolated skill, such as the ability to do jigsaws, but he retarded in all other areas. Many different combinations of these skills will be found within one class of autistic children of similar age and it is essential not to attempt to treat every child in the same way. Care must be taken to ensure that each child is spoken to and given work to do at a level appropriate for his development in each particular area of ability.

For this reason it is rarely possible to teach successfully a group of children together as a class. It will usually be found that some children will be able to understand the lesson and will be interested and alert, while others, for whom the content of the lesson is incomprehensible, will quickly become inattentive and revert to ritualistic or disruptive behaviours.

In the case of children who possess a few isolated skills it is important that these do not become the sole activities expected of them. Leaving a child to repeat the same puzzles or bead threading task day after day may keep him quiet and occupied but is unlikely to be of much educational value. The teacher may find it useful, however, to use these particular activities as rewarding events to increase other more constructive behaviours.

The teaching situation also needs to be organized so that the child can concentrate fully on the teacher and the materials. Autistic children are often highly distractible and have a very short attention span, especially when given tasks in which they have little interest. This is the case even in those children who may spend hours absorbed in some seemingly meaningless activity such as spinning or flapping, or in more creative activities which they particularly enjoy, such as form boards or sorting materials.

In order to begin teaching formal skills it is necessary for the teacher to have some degree of social control over the child if he is to learn to concentrate on both the teacher and the materials presented to him. To achieve this it is first necessary to establish at least short periods of sustained eye contact and also to get the child to sit at his desk for a brief period. The child is more likely to sit at a desk with his teacher if the materials used in teaching are both stimulating and interesting for him and are at a level suited to his abilities. Too simple a task will rapidly result in boredom and inattention; too difficult a task will lead to frustration and irritability. Attention to a task can also be more easily achieved if other distractions in the room are kept to a minimum. For this reason the work areas of the room need to be kept apart from more active play areas. Enticing views of swings or other children playing should be screened from view. Irrelevant materials on the desk should be removed so that attention can be focused on the teaching materials. For very hyperactive and distractible children, even these conditions may not be sufficient. With these children, working in a small quiet room, such as a side office, may be preferable to attempting to work in the busy classroom situation with its many distractions. Once the most suitable work conditions have been determined for each child it is then possible to begin more effectively to build up skills and eliminate problem behaviours.

5. Breaking down the task into manageable units

Before teaching a new skill which is not already in the child's repertoire, whether it is a simple task like eating with a spoon, or more complex behaviour such as learning to talk, it is important to break the task down into smaller stages, each of which can be taught individually. Let us take for example, the case of a disruptive child who is deficient in several important skills, such as the ability to follow instructions, to sit at his desk for any length of time, or to attend to teaching materials presented to him. In order to deal with such a problem it is necessary to work firstly on one particular aspect of the behaviour, such as the inability to sit on command. Even this seemingly fairly simple task of sitting at a desk can be analysed and broken down into much smaller stages, each of which can be taught in turn. For example:

(a) Going towards the desk on the command "Sit down",
(b) sitting down in the chair,
(c) remaining seated for a short time.

Only when all these behaviours are well established is the teacher in a position to begin presenting teaching materials to the child and in the case of a child with little language and few social skills each stage in this behaviour may have to be taught individually. One would first of all show the child that the command "Sit down" was the signal for going towards his chair. This would be taught initially by using physical guidance to propel the child in the correct direction while repeating the command "Sit down". Any attempt by the child to move towards the chair should be immediately praised and rewarded by the teacher. The rewards used would consist of anything which the child particularly enjoyed. The direction to sit would be given many times until the child was able to associate the spoken word of his teacher with his own action of sitting down. The physical guidance used to direct the child at first can be gradually withdrawn as he begins to understand what is required of him. Every co-operative response which the child makes should be praised and rewarded. Once he approaches his seat on command and sits without any physical help from his teacher, the time he is required to remain seated can be very gradually extended from a few seconds at first to a period long enough for formal work to be attempted.

In a similar manner many problem behaviours can be broken down and eliminated in small steps rather than as a single behaviour. A child who is very destructive in the classroom unless closely supervised can be gradually encouraged to spend longer periods of time on tasks alone without destroying the materials he is using. The teacher might begin by giving him a very strong wooden puzzle or form board or similar task which he particularly enjoys. If he places the pieces of puzzle appropriately without biting or breaking them he should be rewarded and praised by the teacher. If, on the other hand, he attempts to destroy the materials they should immediately be removed for a short period before he is allowed to continue playing with them. As the child comes to enjoy a variety of such tasks and also to respond to the praise of his teacher for co-operating in this way, slightly less robust materials can be introduced. When the child is able to work well with these, the teacher can then begin gradually to reduce his direct supervision of the child until he can eventually be left to work alone with even easily destructible materials, such as books, without tearing them.

As the amount of time the child spends in using play and teaching materials appropriately increases, the time he can spend destroying such materials will consequently decrease. This rather obvious fact is nevertheless an extremely important aspect of management for the teacher to be aware of, for problem behaviours cannot be effectively removed unless they are replaced at the same time by other more acceptable activities. It can never be assumed that just by removing problems the child will automatically replace these by desirable behaviours. In almost every case appropriate behaviours will also have to be taught. If the teacher works on the gradual increase of positive behaviours at the same time as the gradual reduction of problem behaviours the child will learn much more rapidly what is required of him.

II. Selection of Techniques

Having identified the particular problem areas to be dealt with for each child, the next step is to decide upon the most effective method of treatment to use. There are a variety of different techniques which can be employed to build up skills and to reduce problem behaviours, and the decision to use one method rather than another will depend very much on the teacher's initial analysis of the problem. Often several methods may be combined to deal with a single problem more effectively.

(a) Altering the consequences of the child's behaviour

Many problem behaviours can be effectively controlled by avoiding the occurrence of circumstances which are found to cause or precipitate such behaviours. For example, as already discussed, boredom frequently plays an important role in the emergence of disruptive, aggressive and ritualistic behaviours. Once the child is fully occupied such problems frequently decline without any further intervention. In other cases, however, it may be more efficient and practicable to alter instead the events which *follow* the child's behaviour. If the teacher is able to reward appropriate and desirable behaviours in a way which is enjoyable for the child, such behaviours are more likely to occur in future. Thus, if a child who is just beginning to play with other children is praised and rewarded, perhaps by a hug or tickle from the teacher, or by some other activity which he enjoys, for each friendly approach to another child, the frequency of such interactions will increase. When building up complex skills in this way each attempt by the child to co-operate, no matter how small, should be rewarded at first, but with time constant encouragement should become less necessary and approval may then be given for gradually more complex behaviours.

In a similar way undesirable behaviours can be removed by ensuring that the consequences of these behaviours are not pleasurable for the child. Most children, whether they are autistic or not, dislike being totally ignored, and attention from an adult can be a very powerful motivating factor. For example, James, a boy of 7, whose language was otherwise very limited, could rapidly discover what phrases most annoyed other people. Once he had found a particularly infuriating phrase he would repeat it frequently. To his extremely houseproud mother, for instance, he would repeat "Dirty Mummy" over and over again until she was so enraged she would resort to scolding and smacking him, all to no avail. She found it extremely difficult not to react to his remarks but eventually she did manage to ignore them and at the same time began to increase her attention for appropriate speech. After a short time the child ceased to taunt his mother with this particular phrase, and new and provocative utterances which he tried from time to time were dealt with in a similar manner, until this behaviour disappeared completely. It was obvious that scolding and even physical punishment did not act as a deterrent to this boy, whilst ignoring him produced a rapid change in his behaviour. It is always important when working with autistic children not to assume that certain consequences will automatically be rewarding or discouraging for the child. It is only by carefully observing what happens to a particular behaviour when different consequences are employed that the teacher can be certain of the events which act as rewards or deterrents for an individual child.

Altering the consequences of undesirable behaviours can be used to remove many problems, but, as stated earlier, it is important that the child also earns rewards for desirable behaviours at the same time. This is especially effective if the behaviours encouraged are in direct competition with those being discouraged. For example, if an aggressive child is rewarded and praised for sitting and working quietly at his desk, whilst attacks on other children are consistently discouraged, the amount of time he will spend on appropriate school activities will gradually increase. As long as he is involved in constructive tasks he will simply not have a hand free to hit other children or pull their hair.

When building up these alternative desirable behaviours it is important that the rewards used are selected carefully according to the child's own likes and dislikes. Sweets, for example, are not always liked by autistic children, and in fact food rewards generally are best avoided. They can actively interfere with some behaviours such as learning to talk, or teaching the child *not* to eat with his fingers. They are not always readily available and are also bad for the child's teeth. With children who show obvious enjoyment of certain activities—listening to music, playing with water or watching television, it is an easy task to use these events as rewards. If, however, the child seems to derive little positive pleasure from such activities, it may be necessary to use as a reward those behaviours which the child reverts to when left alone. This may be scribbling or drawing or perhaps something as constructive as doing jigsaws. Even allowing the child to sit doing nothing or letting him spend a short time in milder ritualistic activities, such as spinning or flapping, might be used to reward previous co-operative activities. Whatever other rewards are chosen, praise and normal social rewards such as smiles or cuddles must always be given at the same time, for by this means it is hoped that eventually the child will learn to work for, and to value, social rewards alone. To be effective rewards should also always be given, at least in the early stages of teaching, *immediately* the desired behaviour occurs. In this way the child learns to associate the reward with that particular behaviour and thus will be more likely to show that behaviour in future.

(b) Facilitating communication

The inability of many autistic children either to make themselves understood or to understand others' attempts to communicate with them is, as previously mentioned, frequently the cause of many temper tantrums and other disruptive behaviours in the classroom. To avoid such problems, as well as making the task of teaching easier, the teacher needs to be aware of the extent of the child's language difficulties and to take steps to overcome them. Many autistic children, although unable to talk, may understand at least part of what is said to them and with such children the obvious aim is to develop the child's use of language. Other children may be able to echo many phrases perfectly but actually understand very few of the words they can say. Here increasing the child's understanding would be the immediate goal. Because autistic children frequently make effective use of non-verbal or contextual cues when they are spoken to, it is often easy for the teacher to assume that the child understands far more than is actually the case and consequently expect too much of him. Children may often seem to understand many commands such as "Get your coat", "Sit down for dinner", "Put your chair away", whereas in fact they are only copying the other children or responding to certain gestures by the teacher.

If an accurate estimate of the child's level of understanding is to be gained, it is important to determine whether he can understand instructions in the absence of additional cues such as gestures, pointing or looking in the right direction, and in the assessment of the child's comprehension, the teacher should deliberately avoid giving such cues.

For children who are limited in their understanding of speech the teacher should make as much use as possible of every modality when conveying information and instruction to the child. For instance, the instruction to copy what the teacher does might be conveyed by a simple phrase, as well as by showing the child the action to be copied, guiding the child's arms or legs through the necessary movements, giving explicit facial expressions of approval if the child co-operates, and correcting his actions both verbally and physically if he misunderstands or does not co-operate. Initially all communication must be simple, deliberate and emphatic. The teacher's speech to the child needs to be almost telegrammatic and to convey only the essentials of the message, such as "Johnny, do this", or "Johnny sit", or "Johnny, no flapping". Irrelevant words which add little to the meaning should be omitted at this stage to avoid confusing the child. Expressions of pleasure or disapproval should be emphasized; a fleeting smile or a murmured, "good", is unlikely to be effective if the child is hardly even aware of it. What is needed is a broad expression of pleasure directed at the child and accompanied by hugs and verbal praise and encouragement. Gestures used should be simple and explicit—pointing towards the child's chair, tapping the table to direct his attention, hand gestures to demonstrate turning jig saw pieces over and so on.

(c) Graded change

Autistic children are often extremely rigid and obsessional in their behaviour. This can cause many problems in the classroom if the usual routine is disrupted in any way. Often the teacher may be unaware of quite how rigid the child's behaviour is because of the normal day-to-day routine in the classroom. Only when a change becomes necessary, such as a new route to another classroom because of builders in the school, or a change in daily routine caused by rehearsals for the school concert, may the full extent of the child's rigidity be apparent.

The treatment of such rigid behaviours should proceed in a gradual step-by-step manner with the teacher very slowly introducing small changes into the daily routine. For example, Charles, a boy of 12, became very rigid about having his lunch at exactly 12 o'clock. To deal with this he was first given lunch a minute or two earlier or later than this time. These small variations were not noticed by him and so, gradually, the time interval was extended until he was able to tolerate longer and longer delays before lunch was served. Clive, a 10-year old, who insisted on everything being always in exactly the same place and became very upset if they were moved, was treated in a similar way. Objects around the house and classroom were moved at first by an imperceptible amount each day. As he was not upset by this the changes were gradually made more and more obvious until he could cope with quite major alterations in his environment without upset.

In other cases it may not be possible to alter the child's environment without his noticing. In this instance the change itself or the consequences of the change should be made as rewarding as possible for the child. For example, take the case of a child who insists on sitting in exactly the same spot at every meal. If he allows his chair to be moved slightly at mealtimes without making a fuss he might be rewarded by going out to play a little earlier. If changes are not tolerated in the daily timetable, favourite activities can be substituted for other lessons and once the child becomes involved in something he enjoys doing he is less likely to insist on a return to the former routine.

Children who are very rigid about the type of food they will eat can also be dealt with in this way. In some instances it may be possible to mix tiny portions of a new food in with the child's usual meal and thus introduce a more balanced diet by disguising the food. In other cases this may not be possible if, for example, crisps or sandwiches are the only solid food readily taken. Here it may be necessary to insist that the child takes a tiny portion of a new food before he is allowed to eat his normal meal. Initial resistance is usually fairly easily overcome when the child realizes he only has to take a very small amount of the newly introduced food, such as half a teaspoon of soup, before his regular meal. Gradually the amount of new food given before the crisps or sandwiches can be increased or the proportion of new food mixed with the usual meal can be increased until the child is taking a more balanced diet. Provided such changes are introduced gradually and desirable, alternative activities are available, the child may even begin to enjoy variations in his routine instead of merely tolerating them. Gradually, larger and larger changes can be introduced into the child's whole environment so that when new circumstances cause a change in routine, tantrums and anxiety are less likely to occur. It is important, however, that every one involved in the child's management should be continually alert for signs that new routines and obsessions are developing and that these are modified as soon as they appear. Introduction of as much variety as possible into the classroom situation both in terms of the physical environment and the daily activities help to prevent the formation of new fixed routines.

The principle of the gradual introduction of changes into the obsessional child's environment can also be very successfully adapted to the child who carries or collects special objects. This obsessional attachment can interfere with many classroom activities. If the child carries a small object, such as a piece of paper or a leaf, the interference may not be great. However, if the child insists on always holding a large box in one hand, it becomes virtually impossible for him to take part in many classroom activities. Attempts to remove such objects usually result in temper tantrums and complete disruption of ongoing activities. Such attachment can, however, be effectively reduced in many cases by gradual withdrawal of the object by a reduction in its size. Andy, a 5 year old boy, had insisted on carrying his large cot blanket at all times since the age of 18 months. He refused to part with it for washing and as it was so large it interfered considerably with any tasks where he needed to use both hands. His mother began to cut the blanket down by a few inches each night and after only a week the blanket measured 2″ by 8″. After 3 weeks it consisted of five threads knotted together. Andy then began to leave these around the house and did not become upset when they were lost. When he began to carry other objects such as plastic buses and postcards these were dealt with in a similar way. However, progress was much faster with these new objects and Andy showed no distress when they were reduced in size. At the same time the parents began to concentrate on providing other activities for him and keeping him occupied as much as possible during the day. He now shows no objection to parting with objects he is carrying and they no longer interfere with other activities.

This method has also been used for children who carry pieces of leather, string, belts, elastic and so on. It achieves rapid results without causing distress to the child but is, of course, limited to objects which are physically capable of being cut or taken to pieces. Some objects like tin cans cannot be easily reduced and in other cases the child may notice any change in his object, however slight. Here it is preferable to reduce the object attachment by gradually decreasing the amount of time the child spends with it. Provided the child is parted from the object for only a short time when he is involved in doing something he likes, say eating, or playing on a swing, this is unlikely to cause much distress. The object should be placed where he can see it and returned to him at the end of the activity. Very gradually the child would be required to spend more and more time on certain tasks before the object was returned, his attempts at co-operation during the time spent without the object being warmly praised and rewarded. The teacher would then increase the range of activities the child was able to complete without it, rewarding all tasks which competed with its presence. In this way the amount of time the child spends on co-operative and constructive activities can be increased and the time spent with the object correspondingly decreased until its presence does not interfere with classroom work in any way.

Many autistic children show irrational fears of objects or situations. These may be very short-lived and change from day to day but more often they become firmly established and lead to a restriction of the child's activities. Such fears can also be treated by adopting the graded approach technique. The child's introduction to the feared object must be brought about in very small stages keeping the time of exposure very short in order to reduce anxiety to a minimum. When dealing with phobias in this way it is always important to allow the child to become thoroughly relaxed and free from fear at each stage of treatment before progressing further. Attempting to move too rapidly from one situation to the next can result in an increase in fear and greater reluctance than ever to approach the phobic object. Whenever possible, exposure to the feared object should also be combined with some other pleasurable event. For instance, Peter, an 11 year old, had an acute fear of balloons which made the period around Christmas very difficult, as he would run screaming out of any room in which a balloon was to be found. Several months before Christmas he was encouraged to join in various ball games. Hard balls were used at first and then inflatable plastic ones. He then progressed to playing with bubbles and later plastic balloons which were made from a kit and did not burst. Gradually, partly blown-up balloons, which would not burst loudly, were introduced and finally fully blown-up balloons. Only when the child showed no anxiety with one set of materials were new and progressively more balloon-like objects introduced. By Christmas he was blowing up and bursting balloons himself without fear.

Similarly 5 year old Timothy's fear of baths were overcome by allowing him at first to play fully clothed in an empty bath. Gradually his clothes were removed and the water level increased until he could be washed normally in the bath and could also be taken swimming in public baths with the school.

Many fears can be dealt with in this way. Tony's phobia about using the lavatory anywhere except at home was dealt with by bringing his old potty to school. He used this first in the classroom and later it was removed to the toilet area. Use of the potty was warmly rewarded by his teacher. When he was using the potty regularly in the toilet area he was then put on the children's lavatory. He used this without any distress and from then on used any other lavatory without fear.

(d) Modelling

Normal children learn many skills by watching and imitating other children and adults. In autistic children, however, this spontaneous imitation is generally much reduced. Before teaching an autistic child complex imitative skills such as speaking or gestural communication, it is often necessary to begin by teaching more generalized imitation such as body movements. When doing this the teacher should act as a model for the child, guiding him gradually through the movements until each is learnt. As always, this would be done in a step-by-step manner, starting by teaching the child how to copy gross arm movements like clapping or waving in response to the command, "Do this". A second adult is often a great help in such a situation to guide the child physically through the actions. Each attempt to co-operate would be rewarded and praised and the physical guidance gradually faded out until the child was imitating on his own. Gradually finer movements could be used, such as touching the face or opening the mouth, until the child was able to imitate mouth movements which are an important early stage in learning to talk.

Modelling can also be an effective way of dealing with phobias in autistic children. Thus the child might watch another person with the feared object or in the situation he fears. Gradually he can be drawn towards the object whilst his anxiety level is kept low by distracting him at the same time with something pleasurable—letting him hold a favourite toy, for example. The child should then be encouraged and rewarded for getting nearer and nearer to the object and finally for touching and playing with it. Andrew's lifelong fear of hair washing was dealt with initially by increasing his general imitative skills. He was then taught to copy his mother bending over a basin. After a time he began to copy her having a little water poured on her head. The amount of water was gradually increased and later shampoo introduced. Finally the child allowed his father to wash his hair at the same time as his mother washed hers.

(e) Active involvement with the child

In order to reduce the stereotyped and ritualistic behaviours which are typical of an autistic child, it is important that adults involved with the child should provide as much stimulation and pleasurable interaction with him as possible throughout the day. Every opportunity should be seized to draw the child into more normal activities, interrupting manneristic behaviours and endeavouring to provide a pleasurable alternative to his solitary activities. At first this might be done by intruding into the child's routine and making it necessary for him to interact at least briefly with the adult before being allowed to continue with his ritualistic actions. This is especially useful for very withdrawn children who have few alternative behaviours. For example, Anne was a child of 6 who made very little contact with adults and spent most of her time spinning any objects—from toy cars to flower pots—on the floor. To reduce this behaviour her teacher began to approach her at frequent intervals and deliberately stop her from spinning. At first this resulted in a temper tantrum but as the object was always returned to her after a brief period she began to resist less and less. This continued removal and then handing back of the object eventually resulted in Anne looking towards the teacher and holding out her hand for the object each time it was taken away. In this way she was taught to make direct eye contact with the teacher in order to be given back her object. Later she also learnt to use a few simple sounds to "ask for" her object. As her communication with adults increased, however, her need for her object became less and less. She began to spend long periods without it and instead spent more time in contact with other people or in more appropriate play activities.

III. Monitoring

When a systematic breakdown is made of a child's problem behaviour, noting events that precipitate it and behaviours of others that sustain it, it is probable that manipulation of one or both of these will result in a change in the child's behaviour. However, it is inevitable that sometimes mistakes will be made and the wrong conclusions drawn about what is causing or maintaining the problem behaviour. If the child's environment is altered on the basis of observation and the problems still do not decline, then a wrong deduction has been made and the situation has to be re-analysed. For instance, a 7 year old's severe temper tantrums were thought initially to be predominantly attention seeking, and attention was therefore withdrawn from him immediately he had a tantrum. After several weeks, however, the rate of tantrums had not decreased. Since merely withdrawing attention from him was clearly not working, it was decided to remove him instead from the classroom to a small sideroom where he could not make so much noise and was unable to throw himself around or to break or damage ornaments. This reduced the frequency of tantrums almost immediately and they have since been maintained at a low level.

Although this example shows that the original treatment decided upon does not always work and may occasionally have to be changed, it is important to continue a regime long enough to establish that a change for the worse or no change at all is a permanent situation and not just a result of the new conditions. Behaviours like temper tantrums which are suddenly ignored, for example, when they had formerly been given attention, will rapidly increase in frequency at first, as the child tries harder and harder to gain attention. However, this is a purely temporary situation and the shouting and crying will soon diminish as the child learns more appropriate ways of gaining adult attention. It is important to try a new approach long enough to decide on the permanency of the behaviours. Ideally this time period should be specified when the new conditions are applied, not halfway through a new treatment plan.

In order to show how a behaviour is changing it is necessary to keep careful records of the times and lengths of the occurrence and how changes in plan affect this. Records do not need to be complicated—just keeping simple counts of, say, how many words the child is using or how many tantrums he has each day, is usually quite adequate. They should not take the teacher more than a few seconds at a time to fill in, and, if kept regularly, they are an invaluable source of information on how the child is progressing, and on the effectiveness of the training programme. For example, Jenny's problem was running away from the playground. Whether this was for exploratory reasons or a means of arousing the fuss and excitement that resulted when she did get away was not known. Initially teachers on playground duty kept a note of the number of attempted escapes made each breaktime for a week, to show how often Jenny was trying to get away, and whether this occurred with particular members of staff. At the end of the week the records were examined and it was decided to try bringing Jenny in from the playground each time she attempted to climb the wall. This had to be done with minimal excitement and Jenny was kept in what was presumed to be a disagreeable situation (a chair in a corridor) for 3 minutes. Records were kept continually and it was soon found that Jenny was spending all her time inside the school and was attempting to escape the moment she was let into the playground. Thus it was obvious that, for Jenny, sitting in the corridor was preferable to being out in the playground. The chair was therefore moved to a corner of the playground and Jenny made to sit there each time she tried to escape. This dramatically reduced the number of attempts to climb the wall. In addition, staff were asked to try to involve her in ball and chasing games at times when she was standing unoccupied. This again caused a reduction in the frequency of escape attempts.

IV. Building Positive Behaviours

Just as undesirable behaviours can be controlled by careful structuring of the child's environment, so too, desirable behaviours can be fostered and skills built up.

(a) Language and comprehension

Once basic imitative skills have been established work can begin on teaching the child to use simple words or sounds to indicate his needs. If the child is already able to make some sounds the frequency of these can be increased by ensuring that he always makes some attempt to ask for what he wants rather than just letting him take the objects himself.

For example, if a child has learnt to use a sound to ask for a particular object, say "b" for biscuits, he can be encouraged to use the sound as much as possible by withholding the biscuit until he does so. The teacher would demonstrate how to form the sound, physically manipulating the child's mouth if necessary until he learns that saying "b" always results in his gaining a biscuit. This can then be extended to many situations: "ow" for "out", when he wants to go out to play; "k" for "kiss when he wants to be cuddled and so on. As his range of sounds increases they can be put together, for example, "w t" for "water", or "k a" for "car" and so on.

At first even very primitive attempts by the child to make an intelligible sound should be encouraged by praising him and immediately giving him the object he wants. Later the teacher can begin to prompt the child to use sounds which resemble more and more closely the name of the object. Gradually the amount of prompting can be reduced until the child is able to name objects appropriately without help. For example, one boy of 8, Billy, had never imitated sounds and had no words at all though his comprehension was quite good. His mother taught him to imitate sounds initially, using physical prompts to help him position his mouth properly to form the correct sounds. After only a few months he had a labelling vocabulary of 40 words and sounds and could use them to ask for things he needed. It was also found, in addition to this, that his severe temper tantrums declined rapidly as he learnt to express his needs.

When words are being used well simple phrases can then be taught and it is important always to try to build up the child's use of more complex speech, rather than to allow him habitually to use very simple or idiosyncratic utterances.

If a child shows no use or understanding of speech it may be more useful to teach him to use simple, concrete gestures instead. At first physical guidance will be necessary to teach the child such actions as pointing or signalling his need to go to the lavatory. Gradually, as in previous imitation training, the amount of physical guidance can be reduced until the child is able to perform these actions on his own.

Occasionally an autistic child who understands no verbal speech at all may be taught the meaning of written instructions. David, a very bright 6 year old boy, was unable to follow any gestures or verbal commands or even respond to his own name despite several months of intensive training. He was quickly taught, however, to recognize written words. He learnt first to match pictures to pictures, then words to words and finally words to pictures. Eventually he was able to match single words to a wide variety of objects and then two or three word phrases such as, "big ball", "box in cupboard", were introduced. These written phrases were then used to teach him to run simple errands around the house or classroom, such as "Get Sarah's coat" or "Fetch the jigsaw". This gave considerable pleasure to the child and for the first time provided his teachers and family with a means of communicating with him.

(b) Building up play behaviour

Children who are very limited in their language ability will obviously be very handicapped in any task where imagination is required and autistic children frequently show very little enjoyment in playing with toys alone or with other children. Presented with a tea set they will usually stack the plates together or spin the cups. They will rarely put the cups on the saucers or pour out imaginary cups of tea. They are more likely to spin the wheels of toy cars than to push them across the floor and there is generally little interest in toy furniture or dolls. The lack of ability to play appropriately causes many problems in the classroom, and in free play periods particularly, the child is very likely to become bored and frustrated. Even the most handicapped children, however, can be *taught* to play appropriately. Teaching can begin in a very simple way such as providing the child with a miniature carpet sweeper, brush and broom, and teaching him to copy the appropriate actions while the room is being cleaned. After rewarding the child in the early stages for attempts to copy the adult, the imitation soon becomes well established and eventually can be obtained by giving the direction to sweep or use a dustpan and brush. The child is not, however, actually using the objects to clean the room but is doing so when there is nothing for him to sweep up. This is the very early emergence of imaginative behaviour. Later, tea sets can be used, initially teaching the child how to pour out tea and rewarding each step he completes. At first it may be necessary to place water in the utensils to demonstrate how things are poured, but later empty jugs and teapots can be used. Children can also be taught to use toy dolls with obvious enjoyment and invention. The actions the family members will be made to perform are often very simple: lying in bed, having a bath, or sitting on a chair or lavatory. It is rare that more abstract or complicated activities will occur such as "Mummy cooking" or "Going shopping". However, in order to establish some degree of abstract language even the most basic imaginative skills are of considerable value to the child.

(c) Building up co-operative play

Autistic children very rarely play spontaneously with other children, but even very withdrawn autistic children can learn to play co-operatively with another child. This can best be achieved by using a game that the autistic child is known to do well and to enjoy, such as a simple jigsaw or construction sets like building cups. The other child initially used in this situation would be a young normal child, an older autistic child who is already able to understand the task fairly well or a child who has some other handicap but is able to join in some simple co-operative games. Initially the two children should be given half the puzzle or half the cups each so that it is necessary for the autistic child to wait his turn and to rely on the other child before he is able to place his next piece. The game should only be allowed to continue as long as the child waits quietly for his turn and does not grab at the other child's pieces. The teacher can direct which pieces of the puzzle are to be placed next and can also restrain the child from using all his pieces at once. Gradually the teacher can withdraw from the situation leaving the two children to complete the game alone. Simple picture dominoes and "Ludo" can also be taught in this way.

Simple ball games and activities with cars and trains can also be built up in a similar manner. Initially the teacher would be involved in the game, teaching the child to push the car back to him or throw him the ball and later would encourage the two children to go through the same sequence, fading out of the situation himself. Gradually the complexity of the games can be increased and later more children can be introduced until simple group games can be played.

In the classroom many group activities can often be increased by teaching simple musical games or active games like "tag" or ring-a-roses. The autistic child can usually be taught these activities step-by-step, and such games are a useful introduction to early group play with other children.

V. Contact with Parents and Other Professionals

Finally, when devising any programme of management for autistic children it is important to be aware of the need for close contact between teachers and others involved in the child's care. When a treatment plan is implemented it is important that everyone involved in the care of the child knows what behaviours are being dealt with at what time, what strategies are being used and what the next step should be. Unless everyone who has contact with the child reacts in the same way to the behaviours, the situation rapidly arises where the child is having tantrums with some people but not others;

dressing himself in some situations and being dressed in others, and talking appropriately and spontaneously to some people but not others. Even phobias and ritualistic behaviours may occur in specific situations. Thus, it is essential for a treatment plan to be drawn up and agreed on by everyone involved and any changes that have to be made should be discussed at regular and frequent intervals by all the people who deal with the child at school, at home, on the journey between or in other specific situations. If consistent handling is achieved, lasting and progressive changes in the child's behaviour can be rapidly produced and maintained.

Just as one finds that the child may change his behaviour from teacher to teacher and in different situations within the school, he may also behave very differently at home and at school. Frequently one finds that a behaviour is under control in one place but not in the other. A child who sits down and eats with a knife and fork at school may run wild at mealtimes at home. Sometimes the people in one situation may not even realize that a problem exists in the other setting, but more frequently one set of people (and usually the parents) become very discouraged and depressed by their inability to control the child. This is especially so if the teachers are able to cope with their child far more successfully than they themselves. It is most helpful for parents to be able to discuss such worries with teachers and other people involved in the care of their child and it is also important that they are given practical advice on how to bring such problems under control. Sometimes watching the child through a mealtime at school or seeing how a tantrum is dealt with can give them ideas on how to handle the situation at home. Notes between the home and school are also helpful for parents who are unable to visit regularly.

If there is a school social worker she can be a vital link between the school and home situation. This is especially so if she becomes involved with the plans for each child and even actively takes part in some of the treatment programmes. She is then in a position to show parents directly how successful handling can be achieved in their own home and help them devise programmes to put into practice there.

Other teachers who take children for special lessons need to know the treatment plans that are in operation for each child and how each behaviour should be dealt with—which are being actively fostered, which are being reduced and the methods used. This is of course essential when children move from one class to a new one so that old problem behaviours which have been removed or are successfully kept under control do not reappear in a new situation.

The role of the school psychologist has already been mentioned in connection with the assessment of those children who for various reasons, such as lack of co-operation or severe withdrawal, are very difficult for the teacher to evaluate reliably. Psychological testing can also be very useful in the case of children who possess a very scattered range of abilities, being very poor in some skills but quite proficient in others. Regular assessment of children by the psychologist can also give teachers valuable feedback on improvement in different areas of ability.

Again, psychologists can be helpful in devising treatment programmes and monitoring existing ones. They may also be able to advise on ways of countering problem behaviours or assessing improvement in skills so that teaching can be aimed at the correct level for each child.

It is now recognized that adequate schooling is of paramount importance in helping the autistic child to realize his full potential and to minimize his social, linguistic and behavioural handicaps. Much has already been achieved by teachers in this field but many problems still remain. Greater communication between all disciplines is needed in order to stimulate research into the most effective methods of educating autistic children, and of overcoming the numerous problems encountered in their teaching. A pooling of the knowledge and skills of teachers, speech therapists, psychiatrists, social workers, psychologists and parents, derived from their experience of, and research with, autistic children, will ensure that these aims are achieved in the shortest possible time.

CHAPTER 5

AIMS AND METHODS OF TEACHING

LAWRENCE BARTAK and GEOFFREY PICKERING

Introduction

The teacher, faced with the task of teaching autistic children, whether in ones and twos or greater numbers, will often find it difficult to know where to start. Many autistic children seem to be multiply handicapped and present a bewildering array of disturbed behaviours and disabilities which present obstacle after obstacle to attempts to get the child to learn anything. In addition, it is often difficult to establish what it is that the child does and does not know. Children often appear to show marked changes from day to day in their abilities, knowledge and grip on their environment.

While planning is obviously sensible in developing teaching programmes for any children, it is vital in the case of autistic children for the reasons mentioned above. If the teacher is not to lose his way and become resigned to a short-term, moment to moment programme of little more than a holding operation then a highly detailed, well-structured long-term programme is essential for each child. This chapter is aimed at setting out a basic plan for such a programme. Other chapters in this book deal with important aspects of any teaching programme for autistic children such as language training, assessment of the child's disabilities and management of behaviour problems. Here the aim is to provide a general scheme upon which a more detailed programme can be constructed. There are five main aspects to such a scheme. In the first place, it is necessary to consider *goals*. These define the end point of any programme for the child. Here one is considering the aims of the work with the child. Secondly, it is of equal importance to define the *current situation*. This involves consideration of the interests and skills and areas of impairment which the child brings to the school. Whereas the first aspect of the scheme is concerned with the end of the teaching process, the second is concerned with the beginning. A third aspect is concerned with the *methods* with which the child may be brought from his current situation towards the goals which have been set up. Thus, the third aspect of the scheme links the first two. A fourth consideration is the need for *evaluation*. We can systematically describe the problems that autistic children present when they come into a special unit, set more or less realistic goals as well as sensible methods by which to achieve them. However, if evaluation of results of these methods is not attempted, successful teaching is likely to be due as much to luck as to judgement and professional skill. A final consideration of equal importance is to ask what *alternative reasons* might explain the results that are obtained in any programme of special education. The majority of teachers working with autistic children have some kind of theory which underlies the methods which they use. However, it is often possible to get sought-after results for totally different reasons than were originally assumed to apply. Education and medicine are full of examples of teaching and treatment methods which worked but for reasons which had nothing to do with the theorizing which led to their introduction and use in the first place. This chapter will consider each of these five aspects in further detail below. They are likely to be of considerable importance in planning any logical teaching programme for autistic children. There have been many special classes and schools for autistic children set up in the past 10 years. However, the little research that has been done has indicated that there are very few teaching programmes that have been well thought through in all five areas listed here and there are likely to be severe limits to what is achieved as a result. For example, some programmes have failed to pay much attention to the current characteristics of the child as he enters the programme. This has resulted in many children being grossly mis-matched to the methods used for them and the goals set. In consequence, special units either fail to examine results obtained (since many children appear as "failures") or they have to resort to various kinds of logical manoeuvres such as reclassifying children after the event. In one case, a child previously clearly diagnosed as autistic and who failed to show improvement over several years in a special class was reclassified as having a "fundamental disorder of personality". The use of this uninformative label allowed the unit to maintain the idea that they could produce major improvement in all "truly" autistic children and so avoid having to tailor their methods and expectations to the children with whom they were faced.

The nature of autism

Let us conclude this introductory section with a brief examination of some of the features of infantile autism that are of major importance from the point of view of the teacher. Many of these will have been described in other chapters. However, there is some advantage to be gained from a brief over-view at this point.

Infantile autism can be seen as a condition involving multiple handicaps of various kinds. However, many of these occur in other disorders of childhood and are thus not characteristic of autism in particular. For this reason it is better to try to describe the basic nature of autism in terms of those features which are present in autistic children only. We are left with three main groups of symptoms, some aspect of each of the three having to be present by the age of $2\frac{1}{2}$ years in order for the diagnosis of autism to be made.

1. A profound and general failure to develop interpersonal relationships (e.g. lack of eye-to-eye gaze, relative failure to form friendships, failure to cuddle).
2. A delay in language development (generally followed by echolalia, pronominal reversal and paucity of conversation even after speech has developed).
3. The presence of ritualistic or compulsive phenomena (e.g. stereotyped repetitive activities, abnormal attachments to unusual objects and resistance to change).

Underlying these features is a persisting and wide-ranging concreteness in the ways autistic children think and speak. It is easy to lose sight of the fact that when most children learn the names of things or the multiplication tables, they not only know the *content* of what has been learnt but a number of other things as well. These include the *relations* between the things learnt or connections between them, the *uses* to which the learned content can be put, the fact that there are *things to be learnt*, and the fact that there are people *who can teach* the things to be learnt. It seems quite likely that autistic children whose comprehension both of language and of social situations is poor and who think in a very literal, constricted and concrete manner will not incidentally learn any of these things. They *can* learn the basic material itself but may never grasp what it is for or how it may be used. In similar vein, many autistic children learn to read but never understand that reading is for *finding out*, i.e. that one reads to obtain information which may be of use in coping with one's environment.

Accompanying the basic features described above may be a number of others. Most autistic children are of subnormal intelligence as measured on tests involving tasks of a non-verbal nature. In other words, even though their performance on tasks of a visuo-spatial kind (e.g. jig saw puzzles) is generally at a higher level than that shown on other kinds of material such as verbal or numerical tasks, it is still generally inferior to that shown by normal children of the same age. In addition, many autistic children may have very short attention span and can be overactive or else clumsy and unco-ordinated. All of these factors need to be considered carefully in planning teaching programmes.

Setting Goals

This section deals with the selection of appropriate teaching aims for specific children. We are going to consider the problem of setting sensible goals separately from that of studying the child in his present state which we will cover in the next section. In practice they must be dealt with together.

The formulation of realistic goals is largely a matter of keeping in mind a number of important principles while deciding what should be aimed for. These principles are as follows.

1. Assessment of the present state

It is very difficult to set up detailed teaching programmes for any child without careful consideration of his present abilities, handicaps and individual temperamental traits. All autistic children share a severe and long-lasting disorder of understanding of speech and language backed by a general inability to handle symbolic material with ease. However, the specific aspects of language function that are disordered may vary from one child to the next. One child may be unable to associate sounds he has heard with their corresponding visual forms but may be able to generalize from relatively short periods of learning within a single sensory modality such as hearing. Another child, on the other hand, may have unimpaired cross-modal transfer, that is he can easily come to relate visual, auditory or tactile presentations of material but may be unable to generalize even from many hundreds of learning trials. Differences such as these which are common occurrences in many schools for autistic children will require quite different teaching programmes as well as differences in long-term goals. Similarly, careful assessment of the child's non-verbal IQ is necessary. This will enable the teacher and psychologist to evaluate the child's reactions to the kinds of demands placed upon him in the school. Angry, disturbed behaviour may be a sign that he is unable to cope with the intellectual demands being placed upon him. In another child, the same behaviour may indicate the reverse; that is that he is being insufficiently stretched intellectually and that greater demands need to be made. Tantrums, withdrawal and obsessional, ritualistic behaviours are generally more easily understood in the context of the child's IQ, and the total picture will then dictate the kinds of short-term teaching goals to be aimed at. Another factor of similar importance is that of motor competence. Many autistic children are said to be graceful, highly co-ordinated and capable of highly complex integrated movements. However, many undoubtedly have a lot of difficulties which vary in specific features from one child to the next. Some children are unimpaired in movements which they initiate but are incapable of copying movements demonstrated to them by others. Other children can copy to some degree but may be unco-ordinated or partially spastic. There will be little point in making use of teaching methods which require a high degree of visuo-motor co-ordination with children who lack it, for example.

In general, consideration of the child's present characteristics will be most important for setting up immediate or short-term aims. When confronted with a new child, the teacher has to start some-where and whatever is to be ultimately worked towards, something needs to be started and it is such current immediate goals which are particularly dependent upon the present pattern of abilities and handicaps.

2. Findings from follow-up studies

When we turn to longer-term goals, it is possible to make use of findings from a few follow-up studies of autistic children which have been reported. There is now a small but useful amount of informa-tion available which will allow us to relate goals to individual features of the child when he is first seen. For example, recent research has suggested that carefully tested IQ in autistic children is useful in predicting later educational progress. Few children with non-verbal IQ of less than 50 and probably none of IQ less than 40 are likely to make any progress on formal educational tasks such as reading or number work. Of course this does not mean that such children have no place in a special educational setting. What it does mean is that the aims of teaching severely subnormal autistic children should not be primarily directed towards traditional skills (that is if the teacher wishes to achieve his aims with any success). Studies following up autistic children both in Britain and in the United States have yielded very similar results. The child of reliably measured low non-verbal IQ can also benefit from a structured special educational programme although the *way* in which he shows benefit may well differ from the progress shown by the brighter child. The severely subnormal autistic child is likely to show improvement in his social responsiveness as a result of suitable special programmes. This means that careful consideration of the intellectual ability that the young autistic child brings to the school must dictate the relative importance of formal educational goals and social or behavioural aims. Other criteria that have been found to be of value include the amount of communicative speech which the child has at as early an age as 5 years. Where a child has some communicative speech or else has some other partially abstract medium for communication such as complex gesture, mime or writing, it is reasonable to expect far greater language and social development in later childhood than in the case of children who do not have any communicative speech by, say 5 or 6 years of age. In the case of the latter kind of child, long-term goals in the area of language might be limited to the development of *some* kind of communicative code such as a set of signals, signs or single words or phrases. Less emphasis would be placed upon the development of complex syntax, for example. It goes without saying, however, that rapid development of ability might well require the teacher to revise his long-term goals and set more ambitious ones. From time to time, autistic children who have no communicative speech at 5 or 6 years of age, for example, will suddenly acquire it at 8 or 9 with a consequent improvement in the prospects of their acquiring useful amounts of normal language competence with adequate training.

A further research finding that is of interest in setting long-term goals is that autistic children who display the most normal behaviour as adults, often living more or less independent lives in the community frequently showed a common feature in their childhood. This was the development of an awareness of the behaviour of other normal children and a keen interest in it. This was often accompanied by attempts to copy the normal behaviour of other children, frequently during adolescence. This would suggest that those autistic children who display interest in their own behaviour and that of other children may be expected to be capable of relatively good later social adjustment. In turn, this would suggest that such children might benefit from extensive structured programmes directed towards the training of social skills. These could include both social behaviours required in various common situations as well as training in perceiving or understanding the behaviour of other people in such circumstances as public transport and shops.

3. Setting goals in detail

A very common fault of many programmes is that where goals are set out at all, they are specified in inferential and general terms. For example, one special education programme might set out to "promote the well-being of the whole child". Others often specify goals in terms of ill-understood hypothetical processes such as perception, motivation or integration of personality. Even a concept as apparently specific as *language* is vastly complicated, difficult to define and made up of lots of separate processes and behaviour, many of which are themselves barely understood. When aims are set out in such general terms, it becomes very difficult to determine whether they have been reached or not. For these reasons, it is necessary to specify goals in very detailed terms. It is also necessary for similar reasons, to specify aims in behavioral or descriptive terms rather than inferential terms. Where we set out goals such as "integrated behaviour" or "adequately socialized", although different observers may agree that the terms are desirable states for the child to be in, they may not agree about what kinds of behaviour make up the state described. For one observer, adequate socialization may require a child to sit quietly in a classroom and to be capable of going to the lavatory without assistance. For another observer, the same term may be defined by a child being able to express his annoyance with other people through water or doll play. Similarly, the goal of "able to read" may be defined either by a given reading age on some standard test or as ability to recite the text of a particular reading book. Accordingly, it is necessary for teaching aims to be both specific and descriptive. When goals are couched in such terms, teachers are most likely to be able to agree on what behaviours must be shown by the child as evidence of attainment and it is easier to establish whether goals have been achieved. For example, "can correctly produce sounds corresponding to twenty or more lower case letters shown" or "plays co-operatively with other children two to five times per week for at least five minutes" are more manageable aims than concepts such as "knows alphabet" and "well-socialized".

4. Covering all areas of behaviour

It follows from the previous section that teachers need to set goals systematically for all aspects of the child's behaviour. There is no guarantee that progress in any particular area of behaviour will result in progress in other areas. This is probably true of most children but is particularly true of autistic children. A systematic educational programme is highly likely to result in children learning what they have been taught and nothing else, unless specific attention is paid to training in generalization from material taught. If teachers are to concentrate upon fairly specific behavioural goals, as is urged above, then it follows that these will need to be set out for many different areas of behaviour separately. For example, specific goals (both short and long term) will need to be set up for motor behaviour, social behaviour in class, at play, in the home, in public, language (both understanding and production), abstract concept formation, personal independence and hygiene, play itself, visual, auditory and other sensory skills, not to mention more traditional areas such as reading and number work. Within these areas, of course, many specific and separate aims can be set up. Reading requires a vital, but frequently neglected sub-division into mechanical and comprehension skills, for example. It is otherwise very easy to teach autistic children to read and reflect the common finding that they don't understand what they are reading, and that they may not understand that reading is for obtaining information.

5. Specifying staff

A further important aspect of planning a programme is the question of who is to carry it out. Although our present knowledge of autism indicates that special education is the most useful kind of treatment, it does not follow that it is to be carried out solely by teachers. The necessary skills will often be found amongst a variety of other people and it is likely that most progress will be shown by children where the treatment programme is based upon their needs rather than upon the available skills of one or two members of staff in any single professional discipline. Most autistic children have a variety of handicaps and adequate attention to these as well as to the strengths that the child has will usually be obtained by having a well-thought-out team approach. It should, however, be remembered that one staff member will usually need to be most closely associated with the child. As with young normal children, autistic children can benefit greatly from a particular relationship with a specific teacher. Furthermore, certain team members will need to have specialist knowledge and therefore be in a position to advise and direct the activities of other members of the team. However, given that the child can develop a close relationship with a particular staff member and that there is some coherence and direction to team activities, a very wide variety of people may be included. Apart from teachers in the school unit, teachers in nearby schools for normal children are important, particularly for the older child. Other people who might be included are psychologists, speech therapists, psychiatrists, paediatricians, neurologists, general practitioners, social workers, dentists, and most importantly, parents. Each one of these may be thought as having a particular area of experience to offer and of being available to be called on for planning for any specific child's treatment.

Various combinations of direction and execution will occur. For example, on some occasions the teacher might plan activities which the parents and speech therapist may carry out with the child. On others, activities might be planned by the psychologist to be carried out by parents and teacher. The important point is that a multidisciplinary approach should be adopted in which it is recognized that everybody including parents have a part to play and have something of their own to contribute to the programme.

In practice, it will usually be necessary to draw up a list of people able to participate and to meet to plan who is to tackle each of the various problems presented by the child in the light of the competence of each member of the team. It will also be necessary to develop effective ways for the members of the team to liaise with one another during treatment. For example, at one special unit, children carried small notebooks in their pockets which contained instructions and other information passing back and forth between parents and teachers. Whatever means of communication are adopted, it is important that they be effective and used systematically for the benefit of the child.

6. Planning evaluation

Many otherwise well-thought out teaching programmes are severely limited because no decision has been taken regarding when a child should be re-evaluated following his entry into a programme. Most children have regular reports compiled, both by their own teachers and, by head teachers, at longer intervals (as in normal schools). However, it is often difficult for such staff who are in close daily contact with the child to make dispassionate and objective judgements about his development (nor is it necessarily desirable). Objective and detailed re-evaluation of the child will need at least as much assessment as is necessary when he first enters the special unit, and should therefore require careful reporting from the entire team who have worked with the child, as well as independent experts on occasions. Such a comprehensive evaluation needs to be planned well in advance and therefore should be set up as part of the planning of the whole programme for the child. Such re-evaluation might take place at intervals ranging from 6 to 18 months depending upon the child's age, time he has attended the unit and his general rate of progress, for example. When such re-assessments are not planned in advance and carried out, there is a strong tendency for children to drift from year to year in a unit, with staff making general assumptions that progress is occurring in spite of the possibility that it may *not* be occurring with particular children in specific areas of behaviour which are generally overlooked.

7. Planning for data

A final aspect of setting up a programme (which may need to be considered at an early stage) is that of specifying what information needs to be obtained from other people. Many dedicated and experienced teachers of autistic children are considerably hampered in their work because they have little information about the child and have not had the opportunity to work out what information they require. Frequently, a child arrives at a special unit with little more than letters of referral from community medical officers or psychiatrists and these may contain no more information than that the child has been diagnosed as autistic. It is necessary for staff to formulate clearly what they need to know about the child and then go about getting the information. Often the social worker and psychologist will be helpful here by obtaining systematic information from parents and child respectively.

Observation of the Current Situation

Many of the important aspects of this section are covered in other chapters or else have already been touched on in the present chapter, so that we will concentrate on drawing together a number of points to note.

As has been suggested above, observation of the child should be based on several basic principles in order to ensure maximum reliability and validity of information. Firstly, information should be quite specific. Global aspects of a child's behaviour such as *socialization* are obviously important but are best arrived at from a number of more specific measures, each of which can be defined objectively. Use of these allows us to draw conclusions with much greater certainty than if more complex global measures are employed.

Secondly, behaviour should be described using a standardized system. If standard scales are used, children can be directly compared with respect to any particular area of behaviour. Of equal importance is that the use of standard scales allows the child to be reliably compared with himself on a previous occasion. The development of standard scales is essentially a problem of choosing a relevant area of behaviour and then defining various categories of behaviour which are to be recorded. For example, staff might be interested in a child's behaviour in the classroom. Informal observation might have established that autistic children in classrooms are either engaged in activities set for them, sitting unoccupied, moving about the room or engaging in stereotyped repetitive movements. Each of these classes of behaviour would need to be adequately defined, so that whatever behaviour occurred, it would be possible to classify it unambiguously under one or other heading.

Areas of behaviour to be observed

Many of these have been mentioned elsewhere but are summarized here. There are three basic questions to be kept in mind in looking at any specific autistic child. First, what basic skills, knowledge and characteristics of temperament does he have? (In other words, what are his normal aspects like?) Second, what pathological features does he show? (That is, what impairments and symptoms of autism are prominent, and thus what are his *abnormal* aspects like?) Third, how do the child's impairments and basic skills or temperament interact or affect each other? For example, a child has a very good memory for words (normal skill) and is ritualistic (autistic symptom). These features are combined in that he spends much time looking up dictionaries and memorizing word meanings without, however, being able to use his knowledge in conversation.

Let us then briefly list some major areas of behaviour which it is important to keep in mind when assessing the child.

A. Normal skills and characteristics

1. *Motor skills*
   Fine movements, gross movements, co-ordination, motor acts initiated by the child, motor acts copied from another person's movements.

2. *Language skills*
   (*a*) *Speech.* Understanding words, sentences, expression of words, sentences, pronunciation, rhythm and tone of voice, social use of speech.
   (*b*) *Writing.* Understanding and expression through written material.

(*c*) *Non-verbal.* Understanding and expression through gesture, signs, mime, facial expressions.

3. *Social skills*

(*a*) *Mealtimes.* Eating, serving himself, serving other people, relating socially to others during meal.

(*b*) *Home.* Social relationships with siblings and parents, helping with tasks, looking after himself at toilet, bathroom, dressing.

(*c*) *Classroom.* Social relationships with staff, other children, looking after himself (i.e. maintaining activity, fetching own materials).

(*d*) *Play.* Playing independently, playing in partnership with other children, knowing how to play, relating to peers and staff.

4. *Cognitive skills*

Capacity for information (fantasy, imaginative play), attentional skill, sensory-motor co-ordination, transfer from one sense system to another (cross-modal transfer, e.g. auditory-visual transfer), generalization from specific learning experiences, capacity for abstract reasoning with non-verbal (i.e. visuo-spatial) material, capacity for abstract reasoning with verbal material, capacity for abstract reasoning with social material (i.e. perception and understanding of situations and implications of such situations involving people) presented in reality, pictorially or verbally.

5. *Formal skills*

(*a*) *Reading.* Mechanical skill (letter, word, recognition, fluency), comprehension skill (can answer questions on material read, can act appropriately as a result of material read), social skill (uses reading to obtain information for pleasure, for education or for greater social effectiveness, e.g. reading signs on buses and shops).

(*b*) *Number.* Mechanical skill (number recognition, counting, four basic processes), ability to apply himself to problems, social skill (uses number skill to handle money in shops, measuring things or reading numbers of buses or houses).

B. *Impairments*

1. *Social development*
   Lack of expression of feelings, lack of contact with other people. Note whether he depends on adults for approval; more generally, what kinds of things are rewarding for this child?, what situations provoke intensification of social symptoms?

2. *Language symptoms*
   General and detailed features of stage of language development (mostly covered in previous section), presence of echolalia and non-communicative speech, what situations intensify output of echolalia and non-communicative speech?

3. *Obsessional and ritualistic features*
   Attachments to objects, rituals, preoccupations, resistance to change. What circumstances intensify these symptoms?

4. *Motor symptoms*
   Stereotyped movements and activities (e.g. twisting objects, twisting whole body), poor co-ordination, clumsiness, spasticity.

5. *Brain dysfunction*
   Fits, loss of consciousness.

6. *Other behavioural disturbances*
   Tantrums, smelling and touching objects and people, overactivity, short attention span, self-injury, sleep disturbances.

Many of the features in the above lists appear several times. It is also likely that other aspects could well be included. However, both lists should include the majority of behaviours both normal and abnormal which are of importance both for the assessment of the child at any particular stage and also for use as goals in planning a remedial teaching programme.

Methods

In planning detailed teaching methods for the autistic child, it is necessary to remember the general principles which apply to any kind of teaching and areas of behaviour under consideration. Firstly, it is advisable to break down goals into small steps so that the child can attain each part with maximum expectation of success. At one special school for autistic children who were of severely subnormal intelligence as well, staff were attempting to teach them to be independent when in the lavatory. The ultimate goal of efficient use of toilet paper was broken down so that children started learning to wipe semi-liquid paste from one wrist, then learnt to wipe it from the elbows, then from the shoulder-blade, then from the lower part of the back. When they reached the last stage, it was relatively easy to progress to the normal use of toilet paper.

At each stage or sub-stage in such an exercise, principles outlined earlier should be followed. Thus behaviours constituting each goal should be defined in specific, explicit terms, and there should be standardized assessment of these at regular intervals to check on progress.

Other chapters include more detail on these principles as they are relevant to management of behaviour problems. However, it should be remembered that attainment of each sub-stage in any learning programme should be rewarding to the child if maximal learning is to occur and it is necessary to arrange the learning situation so that this will occur. Many autistic children are very frustrating indeed to work with and this often makes otherwise dedicated staff react with annoyance at a child's apparent incomprehension or failure. Where children are occasionally successful in such circumstances staff may not react with sufficient emphasis for the relatively non-verbal child to perceive any rewarding consequences of his effort.

No attempts will be made here to discuss specific methods for teaching particular kinds of material. It should, however, be kept in mind that the *general* problem the teacher is faced with is a relatively non-verbal child who needs to be taught literally every element of his ultimate accomplishment. Autistic children generally do not learn by discovery and seldom make conceptual jumps or generalizations. If presented with a given reading book, a child will most likely learn to read from that book and may be quite unable to read anything else. Therefore, all sorts of material and situations must be included in a comprehensive teaching programme. This means that domestic activities, outings, travelling on public transport, play and going shopping are all vital situations in which structured teaching should be provided. Often children are taken on such "extra-curricular" activities but their experience is unstructured, the activity is probably considered by staff as a "break" or welcome relief from formal school activities, and the child generally learns little. Of equal importance is the fact that in the absence of learning how to exploit and appreciate the situation such as an outing or a free play period, the child does not enjoy it either. In turn, this means that what is construed by staff as a free pleasurable activity period (the model for which is probably that of normal children) is for the autistic child merely a useless period of unstructured and meaningless time wastage. Recent studies of autistic children at play, for example, indicated that relatively few children knew how to play and most spent their time in aimless stereotyped movements. A structured teaching programme is very important. However, it is of equal importance to stress that *all* activities of the child may need to be structured at least initially, so that structured teaching of social relationships with others, behaviour at meals, use of transport, shopping, etc., may all need a structured teaching programme sooner or later.

Structured teaching is a term frequently used and abused and it is advisable to consider it in further detail. Recent research has suggested that structured teaching is more efficient in producing improvement in autistic children than less structured methods. There are several points worthy of note, however. Firstly, the term has absolutely no connotations of discipline or moral overtones. Structuring a child's learning situation does not imply that his behaviour is bad in any sense or that it is disapproved of. It means only that certain constraints are placed on the child's behaviour and that it is made clear in some way what is expected of him. This aspect of structuring essentially amounts to a structuring of his *responses*. A second aspect is that the environment surrounding the child is limited, planned and organized. This amounts to a structuring of the *stimuli* that may impinge upon the child. Both aspects of structuring may be viewed as providing external organization upon the child and his immediate world in a situation where he is as yet unable to organize his own behaviour and environment for himself. Essentially, the whole of socialization of any children could be viewed as a process in which there is a gradual development of internal structuring by the child with the lessening of structuring imposed externally by parents and teachers.

A second consideration is that simply providing structured teaching is insufficient. To be useful, structured teaching must be of *relevant* material. Many autistic children spend a lot of time happily engaged in structured visuo-motor activity involving peg-boards, puzzles, etc. However, this kind of activity is essentially maintaining the *status quo* rather than leading to new learning, since many autistic children are already highly skilled at visuo-spatial and motor activity. It is thus necessary to distinguish between the use of structured activity to stabilize and control behaviour and its use to modify behaviour to produce development. The latter activity will, naturally, depend on behavioural control first having been achieved. However, the point is that while behavioural control is *necessary*, it is not *sufficient*.

Motivation

Motivation both of staff and child in the teaching situation is often neglected or else the subject of unwarranted assumptions. This is particularly so in the case of staff. In most other school situations, teachers are partially rewarded by more or less obvious progress and compliance in the children they teach. In the case of autistic children, this is much less true. Children are often slow to learn, progress may be minimal and they may appear to resist all attempts to help them. There are two implications arising from this. Firstly, teachers need to be constantly on guard against their own frustrations impairing the teaching process. Care should be taken to use simple language with autistic children, particularly when they *don't* understand. And yet it is precisely in the situation of failure that many teachers, justifiably frustrated, will give vent to their feelings and speak to the autistic child in a way that he cannot possibly understand, thereby compounding the failure. We need to remember that we are faced with a child who is very limited in his capacity to understand what he can much more efficiently perceive and remember. We therefore need to maintain very highly trained levels of self control so that the information being given to the autistic child from moment to moment is not only structured, relevant and appropriately organized but also within his capacity to absorb. A second implication is that staff must maintain alternative sources of satisfaction in order to minimize their frustration. Teachers should have well-defined patterns of communication with one another. This means that there should be regular staff meetings in which teachers can discuss their own and one another's activities as well as regular reviews of the progress of individual children. Sometimes such meetings will be best organized as case conferences at which visiting colleagues with additional knowledge of a child may join. Often meetings may take the form of group discussion of methods or aims at which problems can be ironed out. Staff should always have full access to all information about a child. There is no justification for teachers having to work in ignorance of basic data on a child which are kept locked up in a filing cabinet. Staff should always be encouraged to participate in further professional education either via in-service training (e.g. visiting lecturers holding informal lecture-discussions with the special unit) or by secondment to recognized courses in special education held from time to time.

In the case of motivation of the autistic child, it has been noted above that it is important to establish what sort of events are rewarding for the particular child. Normal kinds of motivation should never be assumed. However, once the child's sources of gratification *are* known, they can be used to ensure efficient teaching both of various skills as well as the acquisition of more acceptable motives. For example, a child whose only source of pleasure was withdrawal was allowed to retreat into a small room as a reward for limited contact with an adult. Eventually, social contact with other people became well-practised and could then be used as a reward for more formal language and social learning, as the child had become accustomed to it and no longer tried to withdraw. In general, resistant behaviour on the child's part, such as apparent naughtiness, tantrums, self-injury, or lack of attention may improve when greater attention to what the child finds rewarding is given, better care is taken not to over-stimulate the child and more effort is made to ensure that the child understands what is required of him *and* how he can achieve this.

Evaluation of Progress

This will depend for its success on the adoption of the principles and methods outlined already. The use of expert colleagues to provide further information, the standardized definition of aims and methods of measurement and the adoption of a cool, analytical approach to the child's behaviour with the calm expectation that failure will often occur, are all important. A final point is that where a child has shown definite signs of change over a period of time, it is often useful to ask what possible reasons could account for his progress other than the special educational programme to which he has been exposed. Many children may have shown improvement merely by virtue of having grown older. Alternatively, it may be due to some aspect of the programme that is not recognized by staff, e.g. a child may settle down behaviourally because he is moved to a new room and may like it for some reason that has nothing to do with the teaching. Examination for possible factors such as these is often salutary and is necessary if we are to progress in our understanding of special educational techniques as an "analysable art" in Bijou's terms and as a set of scientific methods to be applied to the difficult but not intractable task of teaching the autistic child.

CHAPTER 6

LANGUAGE PROBLEMS AND A METHOD OF ASSESSMENT AND TEACHING

JOAN TAYLOR

General Introduction

An attempt to set forth the principles underlying a method of presenting a remedial programme to language disordered children is here illustrated by descriptions of selected examples of activities used with the children, with explanations of why the activities were found to be useful. The selection is made from the middle section of the programme, not from the earlier section which deals with attention alerting, nor from the later section which concerns language oriented activities.

Many of the activities described are familiar to parents and teachers who try to help, interest, entertain or educate children with learning or language disorders. The difference lies in the use that is made of these activities; firstly in the careful planning of the programme so that the child is presented with a succession of very easy steps, each activity being only a little "harder" than the one the child has successfully tackled; secondly in the insistence that the situation should constantly be so managed that the child gets the maximum benefit in that he takes himself up the steps and is not helped or carried up by the adult. This will be explained in the descriptions of the games, but a simple instance will illustrate the principle. If the adult shows the child a picture and says, "You find one like this", the adult has done the thinking for the child, and the child is required merely to match similar items. If on the other hand the adult gives the child several picture pairs mixed up, and says,

"What can you do with these?" the onus is on the child to spread them out, scan them, notice that they match together, and make an orderly arrangement of them which demonstrates what he has noticed. The child is then doing more than matching: he is taking the first step towards categorizing.

If these two points are carefully observed the child may begin to develop skills and strategies for learning instead of storing memories of items of perceptual input.

The role the adult plays is crucial to the success or failure of a method which seeks to establish for the child a working set, for this can be done only if the child is allowed to do the work. The adult's role is that of neither instructor nor educator. Sometimes she is a presenter of material, necessary to the situation in order that a succession of simple items may be presented to a child who is so confused by a complicated visual display that he is disheartened and does nothing. Sometimes she is as a teaching machine presenting a series of simple linked items; sometimes a player in a game, keeping the rules until the child learns them; or again the adult may be the encouraging friend, holding the child's persistence for him, enjoying and showing appreciation of the child's efforts, so that through observing her appreciation the child begins to be glad about his own success and to enjoy pitting his wits against simple problems.

This briefly introduces the method used; other comments will be made in the descriptions of the activities. One further point should be made here, that the teacher should be very much on the alert to notice the child's small successes and difficulties because to an experienced teacher these are diagnostic of his disorder and indications of his hopeful chance of eventual progress. She should discuss them with psychologists, and with the psychiatrist and neurologist concerned with the child who will assess and interpret her findings in the light of their own knowledge.

I. Making order

The series of activities first described here concerns making simple order. The earlier series of attention alerting games will have engaged the child in handling and dealing with simple objects, exploring and experimenting with different materials, and perceiving the relationship between objects and containers. He can proceed further only if a relationship with another person is established. The dual purpose of the "Making Order" series of activities is to establish a working set in the child and to promote the first early steps in communication. Working together, two or more people engaged on the same problem, is a pleasant form of communication. I have always found that better results can be obtained if a friendly companionship can be established which respects the child as a person. One is not so much anxiously treating a disordered child as endeavouring to make the acquaintance of the person caged inside.

Five games have been selected to illustrate how teaching apparatus, made up from a few blocks, bricks and beads and other items, or from pieces out of construction sets, can be used to give a child ideas for playing. Many other games can be devised on similar lines. The normal child devises his own little games, but the language disordered child often does not invent and create, and he needs to have ideas about playing presented to him until he develops the ability to entertain himself.

Many of these early activities are very simple, and usually do not take very long to do. Although these children will spend long periods on some mechanical activity, they can attend for only a short time to any activity which requires them continually to scan the material, make decisions as to which piece to choose and what to do with it, keep the purpose of the exercise in mind and the rule by which they are working, and inhibit the continual distraction of irrelevant perceptual input.

It is for these reasons that the teacher must often sit by a child, not directing or interfering with his work, but presenting simple exercises by small steps, and "holding his persistence" for him. Just as an autistic child may need to be taught auditory-vocal word labelling by conditioning methods before he can be taught language, so he has to be taught as it were the "vocabulary" of working. He must be trained to look for likenesses and differences; trained to work to rule; trained to see what is relevant. At first this is done by giving him things which he can handle and place, so that the thing is seen to be done. The "Making Order" series of games begins to establish a working set along these lines.

Simple solid shapes; cubes, balls, cylinders and triangular blocks, may be paired or sorted or matched by colour, ignoring shape, or by shape, ignoring colour. Small counting toys may be sorted into kinds or sorted by colour. Designs or pictures may be used similarly. Most of the children find these activities easy to do. The merit of the activities is not that they teach the matching of items according to their attributes, but that they establish a working set: the child learns to take his box; spread out the contents; scan them and decide how to make an orderly arrangement of them. For some of the activities a piece of "structuring apparatus" is provided. This may be a squared board, a long strip of card, a tray with divisions, or other piece of equipment which suggests or "structures" what the child may do with the items in the box. Sometimes the same collection of material may be used with different structuring apparatus, so that the child must "change set", as when he places the pieces he is matching first in a line on a long card, and then groups them differently on a squared card. It is not helpful to the child's development if the adult shows the child how to use the structuring aid. The child should work out for himself the relationship between the aid and the bits in the box. If he cannot do this he needs to be given a similar exercise in an even simpler form.

1. *"Beads on a rod"*

This is an early "conversation" type of game; the teacher and child are both working together on the same task, taking turn and turn about.

Apparatus. Two wooden blocks with rods fixed in. A box of large beads, square and round, of three colours. (Fig. 1)

Presentation. The child chooses one bead and puts it on his rod and waits for the teacher to have a turn. The teacher makes a point of observing what the child has chosen, chooses the same and puts it on her rod. As the beads build up, the two rods are compared so that the child can see that the pattern is repeated.

Variation. The next time the game is played different colours are

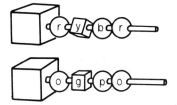

FIG. 1. Beads on a rod (r, red; y, yellow; b, blue; o, orange; g, green; p, pink).

used, or other variation in the material. If the teacher chooses first and requires the child to copy what she does, that is not a variation of this game, but a quite different and more difficult game which requires him to scan and select a matching item.

Comment. This game is a useful starter for children who find it difficult to tolerate the presence of another person when they are playing. In such a case the teacher should sit at some little distance from the child.

2. *"Two on a card"*

This game requires the child to match coloured cubes to coloured squares. Some children do not find it easy to scan a scattered visual display and select what is relevant with regard to both colour and number. Instead of deciding what to do and then doing it correctly first time, they may work by trial and error. Some children find repeated decision-making intolerable, and need to relax their attention frequently. Other children need to be given time for the memory of one card to fade before they are presented with the next card. The game should not be played with quickfire military precision, but more at the pace of two friends having a conversation.

Apparatus. Take ten white cards, $4\frac{1}{2}'' \times 2\frac{1}{2}''$. Cut sticky backed paper, red, yellow, green and blue, into 1 inch squares. Stick two squares on each card, either two of the same colour, or two different colours; some with $\frac{1}{2}$ inch space between, some with the two squares touching. Philip and Tacey's coloured plastic cubes are used.

Presentation. (a) The teacher has the cards; the child has the box of cubes. The cards are given to the child one at a time, and he picks out two cubes of appropriate colour and places them on the squares.

If he makes errors he is allowed to correct himself. The cards when completed to his satisfaction are placed in a row in front of him working from left to right. Some adults find it very difficult to prevent themselves interfering in the child's efforts to come to terms with the simple problems which this game poses.

(b) The child may be given the cards and the box of cubes to work with on his own. Some children, although they can perfectly well match colours, find the organizing of all the bits and pieces very difficult. They should not be shown how to arrange them, but should be given fewer.

(c) The game may be varied on a subsequent occasion by giving the child coloured rods instead of cubes.

It is not a variation on this simple game, but a different and much more difficult task, if, after it has been shown to the child the card is put face downwards. This requires the child first to try to remember a visual display of number and colour, and then to forget it in order to attend to the next item.

3. *"Sort by shape: sort by colour"*

This is an early attempt to get the child to demonstrate that he perceives categories.

(*a*) *Apparatus.* Nine coloured beads: three round, three cylindrical, three cubic: and three little dishes. (Fig. 2a)

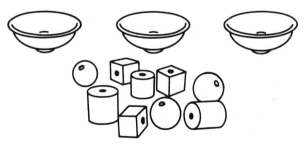

FIG. 2a. Sort by shape.

Presentation. The child is to sort the different shapes into the three dishes. He should work this problem out for himself. If the teacher puts a shape in each dish, she is asking the child merely to match, and she has robbed him of the opportunity to categorize which the game is designed to give him. If she then gives him the same game next day and he does it, he will not be categorizing, but merely remembering what she showed him on the previous day.

(*b*) *Apparatus.* Six beads, in three shapes, round, cubic and cylindrical, and in two colours, yellow (y) and blue (b); also two little dishes. (Fig. 2b)

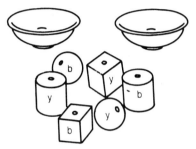

FIG. 2b. Sort by colour (y, yellow; b, blue).

Presentation. This time he is to sort the beads by colour into the two dishes. Again the object of the exercise is not merely to get the beads sorted tidily into two dishes, but that the child should work out for himself the problem presented. He has a dual task: to forget the arrangement in (a), to look anew at his material and work out a new arrangement.

A variation of the game would be to give him a similar problem with different colours, or different materials, or a different structuring device such as a divided tray.

4. "3 cube blocks"

The child is asked to copy the teacher's arrangement of the blocks. This is an early "make and break" game, which uses the same few items in several different ways.

Apparatus. Six small cube blocks, all the same colour, three for the teacher and three for the child.

Presentation. The teacher makes an arrangement of blocks, using one, two or three of them. The child is invited to copy the arrangement. The arrangement of blocks should be left for the child to see. To hide it, or cover it, and expect the child to reproduce it from memory is a quite different exercise. (Fig. 3)

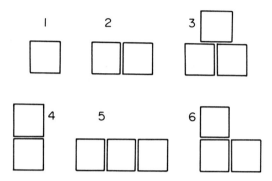

FIG. 3. Cubic blocks.

Some children find it very difficult not to use all three blocks when the arrangement requires only two. Some children want to use all six blocks to make a line or a tower.

5. *"Box of cubes"*

This is a little, informal "conversation" game, and can be played anywhere where there is a flat surface to work on.

Apparatus. A box of 1 inch plain wooden cubes.

Presentation. The teacher builds with seven cubes as shown in the diagram (Fig. 4), and then hands cubes to the child one at a time to put on where he likes. Some children perseverate, building up, or building along; some fill in the corners; some make steps.

If the child continues to build on in a straight line, it is better just to stop the game. Start again another day and alter the playing, so that both teacher and child work on the building, the teacher breaking the perseveration by turning a corner, or working towards a square with four towers. Each time the game is played a different building should be made.

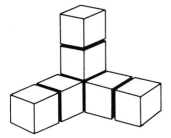

FIG. 4. Box of cubes.

These are only five of a great number of simple activities each of which gives a child the opportunity to make his own observations about collections of simple items, and requires him to place the material in some simple orderly arrangement which demonstrates what thought he has given to what he has observed.

II. Working to rules

The games quoted here are selected from several series which require the child to work with another person to a sequence of rules. The child should pick up the rules by playing the game, just as a child playing "snakes and ladders" for the first time might ask, "How do we play?" and be told, "You'll see as we go". The "structuring devices" which control the situation are the rules of play which both players observe, and which are enforced by the adult until the child remembers and works to the required sequence of action.

Complicated verbal instructions may only confuse the child. One does not explain, for instance, that the players have to take turns, but merely says, "Now it's your turn", "Now it's my turn" until the child begins to take his proper turn without needing to be reminded.

1. *"Ludo"*

The child is required to learn and to use a simple sequence of action.

Apparatus: as in diagram (Fig. 5)
   (i) Each player has a card strip as illustrated.
  (ii) There is a pile of small cards, $1'' \times 1\frac{1}{2}''$, some marked with one small circle, some with two.
 (iii) There is a dish of counters.
 (iv) A few small sweets as prizes.

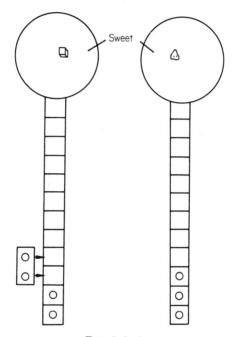

FIG. 5. Ludo.

Sequence of rules for play

Each player takes his turn.
  (a) Picks up a small card.
  (b) Places one or two counters on it as appropriate.
  (c) Places card beside strip and transfers counters to strip.
  (d) Discards little card.
  (e) Sweet is won when the strip is filled.

Wait for the child to do the next step in the sequence, but remind him if he cannot remember the sequence. Some children take quite a long time to learn the sequence of play.

2. *"Colour Lotto"*

This game gives the child the opportunity to say, "Yes, it fits", or "No, it doesn't".

Apparatus

(i) A cloth bag with drawstring, or a covered tin with elastic in the top.
(ii) Pairs of coloured flat shapes: two of each shape, but each shape of a pair is a different colour so that it matches only on one board.
(iii) A board for each player, as in the diagram, with coloured shapes drawn on. This could be made out of cardboard or woodboard. (Fig. 6)

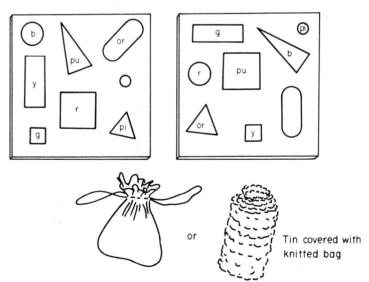

FIG. 6. Colour lotto.

Rules for play

Each player has a board and the players take turns to dip into the bag for a piece. If the player can place the piece, it being the right colour and shape, he puts it on his board. Both players nod and say, "Yes". If it does not fit any uncovered shape on his board, or if it is the wrong colour, he puts it back in the bag, and misses the turn. Both players shake heads and say, "No".

Give the child the opportunity to be the first to "comment" with "Yes" or "No".

3. *"Simon says sticks and rings"*

This is another simple work-together game. The child is required to take turns, infer the rules of play, and to change set.

Apparatus. As in the diagram (Fig. 7). The wooden base is the long strip from a Makimor construction kit, and the twelve green sticks are from the same kit. Twelve rings or beads are also required, and two cloth bags, or covered tins with elastic in the top. Six sticks and six rings are put into each bag. Each player has a bag.

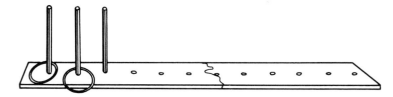

FIG. 7. Sticks and rings.

Presentation. The teacher feels for a stick in her bag and puts it into the base. The child is to find a ring to put on it. He is not told to find a ring, but if he gets a stick out he is told, "No". He puts it back and tries again. When he does get a ring out, he puts it over the green stick in the base.

After a few goes with the teacher finding a stick and the child putting a ring over it, the teacher then produces a ring and holds it ready, expecting the child to change set and see that this time he is required to get a stick. He is not told to get a stick. He is to infer from the situation what is required. The same continues with the teacher producing a ring or a stick in random order, and the child finding a stick or ring as appropriate.

Some children find it very difficult repeatedly to make this simple decision as to which they should bring out of their bag.

Many different games of this type are played, mixed in among the 'Making Order" games. They help the child to use the skills and techniques he has learnt, foster in him an alertness to a whole situation, and help to develop in him tolerance of other people and co-operation with them.

III. Topic and comment

A block may be both a cube and red; a toy may be named as a car and stated to be blue. The three games here described give the child simple ways of making two statements about a single object. For instance, by using sketches and coloured cards a child may describe the toy he wants, and if the child can verbalize, the visual display of the two cards may help him to make a statement in correct sequence of words.

1. *"The triangle is yellow"*

This game requires the child to observe on the card "statements" concerning colour and shape, to put these two together and pick out the "coloured shape" they describe.

Apparatus

(i) Ten cards (4″ × 2″) are prepared. On each of them is an outline geometrical shape drawn and an irregular patch of colour.

(ii) A box of twelve coloured blocks, ten of which match the "descriptions" on the cards as to colour and shape, but not necessarily as to size. The two extra blocks do not fit any card. (Fig. 8)

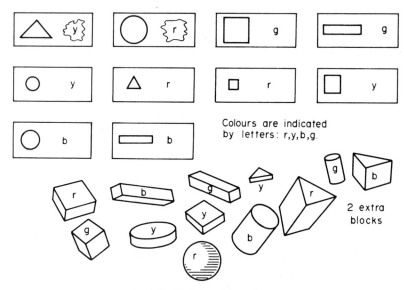

FIG. 8. The triangle is yellow.

Presentation. The child is given all the blocks on a tray. The cards are presented to him one at a time. The child "reads" the card and finds the corresponding block: "The triangle is yellow". A similar game can be made up and given to him as an "occupation", to work out on his own.

What he does should be accepted without correction. If he is "corrected" by the teacher, and subsequently "gets it right" he may be merely remembering her correction. If he is not corrected and on a subsequent occasion gets it right, he has probably worked it out for himself, so that not only has the child learnt to cope with a problem, the teacher also has learnt something about the child.

2. *"The car is blue"*

This game is to the last game as writing is to reading, or as speaking is to listening to speech. The child chooses the "statements" he thinks are relevant to a given object.

Apparatus

(i) Four cards, $1\frac{1}{2}$ inches square, one of each colour, red, yellow, blue, green.

(ii) Four cards, $1\frac{1}{2}$ inches square, each with a black and white sketch of a toy: e.g. car, boat, horse, elephant.

(iii) A tray or dish of little toys, being the toys sketched, each toy in two or three colours, so that there are altogether about twelve toys. E. J. Arnold's *Counting Toys* can be used.

Presentation. A child who has reached this stage in the programme is able to work by himself to instructions given by the teacher, so that after a demonstration of what he is required to do the child may be left to continue on his own. This is a "make and break" game in that the cards are used again and again in different associations.

(a) The child picks a toy out of the tray, finds the sketch card and the colour card, and places them side by side to make a "statement": e.g. (the car) (is red).

(b) An alternative use of the apparatus: the child places a sketch card and a colour card side by side and the teacher finds the toy to match, or shows that there is not one like that.

FIG. 9a.

FIG. 9b.

3. *"Red bridge"*

The child "makes statements" about the attributes of simple objects by choosing cards which "describe" them.

Apparatus

(i) A collection of objects of simple shape. Some are either red or green, of others there is both a red and a green. The diagram shows a typical collection: a square bridge, a round bridge, a hollow cylinder, a cube, a long brick, a triangular brick, a pyramid, prism and round rod. (Fig. 10a)

(ii) Two colour cards, one red and one green, and six other cards with outline drawings as in the diagram. (Fig. 10b)

Presentation. The cards are spread on the table randomly mixed. The child is given one object, e.g. a red bridge. He is asked to find all the cards that are "like" that object.

He may find only the bridge shape and the red, and so has stated that it is a bridge and is red. The cards may be "read aloud". He may notice also that the side is a rectangle and the end a square, and demonstrate his observation by choosing also the cards 2 and 4.

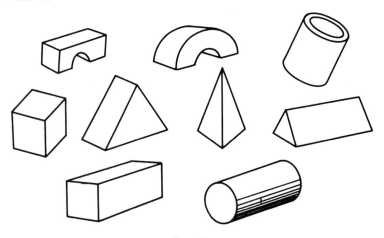

FIG. 10a.

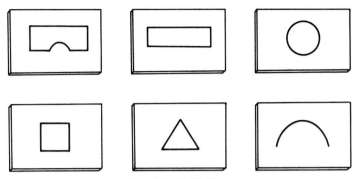

FIG. 10b. Red bridge.

Another game may be played with this apparatus: the child may place several cards and the teacher must find an object which "fits" them all. These games are played in a "conversational" manner, the players talking together and each setting little problems for the other, a kind of question and answer.

IV. Building concepts

The next stage, overlapping with earlier and later stages, concerns the building of concepts. Some of the work, for instance, gives the child a great deal of practice in dealing with such matters as sequencing, categorizing and association of ideas. At this stage the child may be beginning to use words and phrases and this helps to weld and further the learning processes.

Sequencing. The sequencing games include many which require the child to start at the left and proceed one at a time to the right. This habit is so ingrained in us that we sometimes forget that the child may not have it. A simple example is making a row of items of alternating colour, shape or pattern. He may be asked to repeat several times a sequence of two or three items. Games using sequencing memory may be presented which require the child to remember and reproduce a sequence of two or three items, objects, toys or pictures which are shown and then hidden. Seriation games are not included here because few of these children are able at this stage to infer the rule by which a series grows. Many children find the repeated decision-making which these games demand very difficult to tolerate.

Categorizing. These games present a variety of materials which have to be sorted. The child will scan and decide how he can make simple order: making simple sets; sorting by colour and shape; sorting pictures according to common content. For example, animals, buildings, clothing and fruit are some of the easier ones. He may sort by attributes or into classes. He may still need the structuring devices which he used in earlier games, but he is now aware of and is looking for other relationships than similarity of colour or shape. He learns to "make and break" in a different context, in that he learns that items may be arranged in one way and then re-arranged in quite a different way.

Association. These activities ask the child to sort or match various kinds of material according to the more abstract links of association of ideas. He may be asked to match up pairs of things or pictures of things that "go together", e.g. cup and saucer, knife and fork; things which are useless apart, such as lock and key, hammer and nails, lamp and switch; he may be asked to sort clothing for feet, hands, head; things that go in the kitchen or bathroom; things used on the cooker or put on the table; things that belong to mother, father or baby. The material can be presented in very many different ways, not only as a table game of matching. Two or three children may play together according to simple rules of play. For instance, one child may have the "cooker", another may be "laying the table", and each picture that is turned up or toy that is found in the bag is given to the child it "belongs" to.

Concepts. In the earlier activities the child was dealing with things that are present, things that stay to be looked at, and that can be handled and placed. Gradually activities are introduced in which one "ingredient" is not present. "Repeat a simple sequence" is an activity that many children find difficult, for they must hold in their minds, in spite of all distracting visual input, that it is the three items of the sequence that are to be repeated. Cue-matching, substitution and symbolizing activities are also not easy. The child must recall not the object present, but its associated symbol.

A child may be able to demonstrate that he observes the attributes of objects. For instance, he may be able to "state" by selecting prepared cards, that he sees that an object is red and is bridge-shaped, and has a long side and a square end. He may also be able to demonstrate that he remembers that a frying pan is used on the cooker, belongs to mother and is used for cooking sausages. He may be able to remember a short sequence of pictures or coloured beads and reproduce the sequence. Can we get him to do simple tasks which show us that he "has" these concepts? The three games quoted in this section are examples of the kind of games we use in attempting to do this.

We cannot pose the problem to him in words. If we say, "The bridge is red; the block is —?"; or "The iron is Mummy's; the hammer is —?"; we almost give him the answer: he has only to close the sentence with a similar word. So he works out the problems with visually presented material, and when he has finished it he may put it into words if he likes.

Three games have been selected to show this stage of the work.

1. *"See the pattern of the sequence"*

A whole sequence may be laid out in two colours, and the child be asked to build one alongside using two different colours.

A sequence of e.g. two blacks and one white repeated is laid out and the child is asked to repeat it with red beads: he is given beads of two shapes, round and square. He must be allowed to work this out without help. Many simple games can be devised on these lines, constantly presenting fresh material.

2. *"Second red bridge game"*

This requires the child to make a statement about a second object which is analogous to that made about the first.

Apparatus. The same apparatus is used as for the first red bridge game. In addition, to structure the problem, a 6 inch square card is used. This is divided by black vertical and horizontal lines into four squares.

Presentation. The problem is set out as in the diagram:

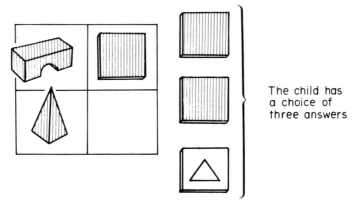

The child has
a choice of
three answers

FIG. 11. Second red bridge.

3. *"The frying pan"*

This game presents the same type of problem as the previous game, but deals with associated ideas instead of attributes.

Apparatus. Use again the 6 inch square to structure the problem, and also a collection of little pictures stuck on 3 inch square white cards. Philip and Tacey publish sets of sticky backed little pictures which cover the vocabulary of their *Story Maker's Picture Dictionary.*

Presentation. Problems are posed by placing three pictures on the square and giving the child a choice of three pictures from which to select one to fill the fourth space.

Examples:

(a) frying pan . . . sausage; saucepan . . . ___?
   Choice of three answers: Mummy, carrot, cooker.
(b) Hammer . . . Daddy; iron . . . ___?
   Choice of three answers: ironing board, Mummy, wall switch.
(c) teapot . . . table; frying pan . . . ___?
   Choice of three answers: sausages, Mummy, cooker.

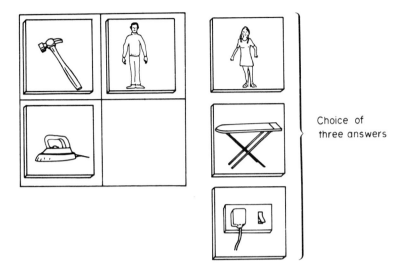

Choice of
three answers

FIG. 12. The frying pan.

We have not described a method of teaching, still less have we outlined a programme of work, but have attempted only to express the principles on which we based a method of helping language disordered children to learn. It is a very rare parent who can give a 2 year old a posting box without showing the child either that the pieces can be taken out, or that they can be put through the holes, who can allow the child the delights of discovery. This is the kind of self-discipline required of parents and teachers who use this method of fostering the ability to learn. The programme of work referred to here is only a part of the whole therapeutic and educational scheme, but the same principles underlie all the day's activities.

CHAPTER 7

ORGANIZATION OF A SCHOOL FOR AUTISTIC CHILDREN

SYBIL ELGAR

According to the dictionary, meanings for the word "organize" include the following definitions: to systemize—to arrange—to establish. Organization appears to me to be controlled by the individual concerned and the circumstances relating to the subject or object to be organized. For example, the organization for a school within the state system is different from the organization required for an independent school. There are no accepted theories nor are there any established rules, and I can only describe how the school at Ealing has developed.

Buildings

In 1965 the National Society for Autistic Children bought a late nineteenth-century house situated near Ealing Common. The house was a well-constructed one with large rooms, a walled garden and, a brick-built annexe containing, at that time, four small rooms. After the usual consultations with architects, Inspectors from the then Ministry of Education, and the subsequent carrying out of extra work and alterations suggested by them, we opened the National Society's first school and I was appointed Headmistress.

Hardly had the school started in No. 10, Florence Road, when the house next door was offered for sale. It was an ideal opportunity to provide more places both day and residential, but funds were limited and it was necessary to raise a mortgage to purchase this house. We now had two houses, No. 10 and No. 8, Florence Road, but as time went on and the existing pupils became older, more applications were received for admission and the need for additional classroom space became all too obvious. Then another adjoining house, No. 12, Florence Road, became available. Once again it was too good an opportunity to miss. We were fortunate in arousing the interest and determination of some good friends and through their efforts at fund raising and the help of some parent members this house was purchased.

The last property to be obtained was No. 6, Florence Road, and it was bought by a Parents Trust formed from some of the parents of children attending the Ealing School. This group of parents organized themselves extremely quickly and efficiently to raise the necessary money for purchase.

This house was bought before April 1971 (at which date all handicapped children became the responsibility of their local education authority) to ensure continued accommodation and education for some of the children at Ealing who were "at risk". That is, the very slow and limited learner and more disturbed child, only able to accept "social" situations for very limited periods and more likely to develop with less demanding academic and social programmes.

Use of Buildings

No. 10 houses the Infant and Junior School and we use three large rooms and a play/utility room for teaching purposes. Twenty-seven children with an age range from 4 to 13+ are divided into six groups with a teacher for each. In this building there is also a dining room, office accommodation and a spare room for psychologists visiting the school.

No. 12 provides extra classrooms and dining room space for senior children, plus other rooms used by the whole school for pottery, laundry, woodwork, art, and a very large room used for P.E., dancing, music, etc. Ten pupils in this house are accommodated in two classrooms and their age range is from 14 to 18 years—each group has a teacher in attendance plus student teachers attending from various colleges.

No. 8 is used as the main boarding department and twenty children live in three self-contained flats with a housemother in residence on each floor. Boarders are selected because of distance or because of particular problems which make it difficult for the parents to cope with their child at home. I live on the school premises and the house staff have direct internal communication to my living quarters should they need to contact me at any time of the night.

The whole of *No.* 6 was not required for school purposes and only the ground floor (completely self-contained) was taken as an adjunct to the school and commenced in February 1970. The accommodation for the children in this house consists of a classroom for the three children of limited ability, a spacious hall used also for a play area, a common-room, a bedroom for three boarders, a kitchen and dining room, bathroom and staff accommodation. The staff in this house consists of a teacher and a housemother.

All the gardens of the four houses adjoin and it is possible to walk through the back gardens from No. 12 to No. 6.

You may remember that I referred to a brick-built annexe at No. 10. During 1971, through the kindness and hard work of local charities and our parents, this building was altered and renovated and a heated and properly filtrated indoor swimming pool installed, which has proved to be a valuable asset.

We now have a picture of buildings, rooms and groups of people, but a building is just a building until children and staff make it into a school.

Staff

My staff have, in the main, been with me for some years and all of them are involved in day-to-day contact with the children—not only teachers and house staff but cleaners, cooks, office staff and the welfare assistant, all take part in a structured situation planned to help our pupils. Teaching staff includes graduates, qualified teachers and teachers holding Montessori diplomas.

In addition to teaching staff we have, as already mentioned, visiting student teachers from teachers' training colleges and one welfare assistant.

Children

The children have all been referred from various centres and have been diagnosed as autistic or psychotic some having additional handicaps such as epilepsy, physical handicaps, brain damage or impaired hearing or vision.

Within the school there are nine teaching groups with a teacher for each group. As far as possible pupils are grouped according to age with a fairly wide scatter, e.g. 4 to 7, 8 to 10, 11 to 13, 14 to 16, etc., but this is not always feasible because of the variance in individual development. For example, a child of 10 just admitted to school for the first time may not be as able or as controlled as a child of 7 who has been at the school for 2 years. Within one teaching group even with similar age grouping, it is highly unlikely that the pupils will all be equally adjusted or equally able, but this situation does not present any insurmountable problem because it is not necessary for every child within a group to be concerned with the same task or occupation at the same time.

Autistic children need to be taught all their skills:

(i) to behave in accordance with accepted social standards,
(ii) to become independent so far as they are able,
(iii) to increase their understanding of language,
(iv) to develop working habits and extend concentration and application,
(v) to acquire academic and occupational skills,
(vi) to play and to organize leisure time,

and these requirements provide a wide choice of activities for the teacher to occupy her pupils with, from simple skills to fuller academic activity.

Although the condition of autism can occur at any intelligence level a number of surveys show a marked bias towards the lower levels of intelligence and the range at Ealing at the present time with non-verbal tests is from severely subnormal to near average with the majority of children in the subnormal range. I have therefore planned the school curriculum at Ealing to help our pupils minimize their disabilities which, I believe, include:

(1) severe retardation in the development of language and cognition;
(2) behavioural abnormalities;
(3) apraxias and problems with co-ordination;
(4) lack of motivation and application.

We work systematically in all situations to extend and improve control, awareness, understanding, vocabulary and knowledge. In our curriculum adequate time is allowed for creative subjects also such as music, dancing, art, handwork, crafts, needlework, cookery and "play" times.

In the same way as with any other group of children, autistic children are individuals, each one with a different personality and a widely varying degree of potential, handicap and behavioural abnormalities. To help with effective learning, I believe it necessary to devise, within the structure of the overall curriculum, separate and particular programmes suited to each child's need and I prepare these for my teachers at the beginning of each term.

All the autistic children I have seen have suffered from linguistic abnormalities. At worst they do not talk at all and at best their speech range is limited, often disjointed and telegrammatic. I do not think that a wordless child can be made to speak but he can, through practical and controlled exercises, be helped with the association of words to objects or actions.

Many wordless children have arrived at Ealing and they have not appeared to understand even simple speech, and it has been my experience that the understanding of words is usually established before their proper use and when the child starts to utter it is in monosyllables with obvious faults in articulation and pronunciation. Of the children at present on roll we have three that remain speechless—a boy of 16, another of 14, and a new arrival of 5.

We concentrate on language development in all situations. Vocabulary is systematically improved by naming objects, articles, people, children, furniture, etc. We teach nouns first because the association between word and object is most obvious. Verbs, modifying, qualifying and positional parts of speech are illustrated by practical actions and once the child is able to use words we introduce phrases, then sentences, always aiming to develop language as a means of communication.

I have found that once the autistic child responds to teaching and starts to use words it is not very long before he will use such phrases as:

"go out please", "more pudding", "go to the toilet",

and various other remarks relating to his immediate requirements. He has been taught these words, understands what they mean and in this connection realizes the usefulness of spontaneous speech and is able to apply the language correctly. Conversely, autistic children often appear to ignore language even when one is fairly sure they understand—they appear either to be "switched off" or aware but disinclined to respond. I believe it is possible to tell the difference between inattention and resistance or confusion and lack of comprehension, and act accordingly either by repetition or insistence until the child reacts, or try again to help him understand what is required.

Behavioural Abnormalities

So far as the teacher is concerned the disturbed behaviour of new entrants is of primary importance. A hyperactive uncontrolled child lacking concentration or any degree of self-organization can quickly disrupt other pupils and the situation can become chaotic.

Attempts to direct, control or organize are likely to promote strong reaction but it must be apparent that if the child is to be taught at all, his behaviour needs to be modified to conform to a more acceptable pattern. It has been my experience that within a structured situation it is easier to control behavioural manifestations and to replace them with more purposeful occupation.

Apraxias and Problems with Co-ordination

Despite dexterity in some ritualistic mannerisms most of the children in my school are not as able in performing and copying more useful movements. Verbal instruction does not always help and the children often cannot reproduce movement from example but need to have their limbs manipulated. In the initial stages they need help in coping with stairs, buttons, clothes, cutlery—they are often not able to ride bicycles, scooters, or to respond to musical games requiring hopping, skipping, stamping, etc., and writing, drawing and figure work are often immature and untidy. As with other children, P.E., rhythmic movement, dancing and swimming, help motor ability but a great deal of individual attention and repetition are needed to help the autistic child develop co-ordination and control.

Lack of Motivation and Application

Autistic children do not learn progressively through their environment and in the initial stages application and concentration are extremely limited. They show little curiosity or interest in new situations and are often reluctant to "try" new work or to accept a different presentation of a familiar exercise. On other occasions a child may "opt out" from any learning situation. I believe structure, firm assessment, clear presentation and steady determination provide the necessary support to help the child develop more positive attitudes and more consistent work patterns.

Admissions to Ealing

All applications for admission to the Ealing School are considered by the school's consultant psychiatrist and myself and interviews are arranged to see parents and children during school holidays. We might decide to accept four or five new children during one term but I only take in one new entry at a time and he is included in my group.

The last ten children admitted to Ealing have been placed in my groups of five or six children and they have responded to the existing control and structure.

It has not been my experience that control has in any way adversely affected an autistic child. On the contrary, I have found the majority of them unable to cope equably with too much freedom and permissiveness.

Our school day at Ealing starts at 9.15 a.m. with a half-hour mid-morning break at 10.30. Lunch time is from 12 noon to 1.30 p.m. and tea is at 3.30 p.m. The children go home or to the boarding department from 3.45 to 4 p.m. and teaching staff are on duty all day and have free meals and refreshments. The children move to different rooms and to different teachers for various subjects.

Boarding Department

At Ealing we try to train our children to be socially acceptable, happy, integrated and, within individual limitations, useful and responsible. The boarding department as a "home" environment is less demanding than the school situation but the structure remains constant.

My house staff appreciate that children need to be "taught" every aspect of living—personal care, domestic chores, to share, to play, to sleep, to eat, and so on. I would not want to understate problems with eating and sleeping or other behavioural abnormalities and I know of no quick "cure" for these ills. Records concerning the development of other children may help as a guideline for action with new entrants but the spur or deterrent for one child may not apply to other children. Indeed, the same child may not react in the same way from day to day or even from hour to hour and a great deal of patience and repetition is needed to help autistic children. Clashes that occur between staff and pupil could possibly be avoided if the child were left to eat with his hands or not eat at all; if we dressed and undressed him, if he were allowed to roam around all night, but such compliance would not in the final analysis help the child. My house staff and I work together to help each child adjust to a more normal pattern and we have a spare room and bed available should it be necessary to move a child into a room alone because he consistently disturbs the other children.

I have found that only experience brings the assurance to be firm in authority, confident and secure enough to know that one is acting in the interest of the child to solve these problems.

Medical Services

We are fortunate in having the services of a G.P. who has his surgery opposite the school. The local school health service of the borough arranges for termly medical inspection of our pupils and for periodic dental checks. The consultant psychiatrist for the school or his representative visits the school at frequent intervals and is available for advice if required.

Play and Leisure

Autistic children need to be taught to play, to play together and to share social situations. Their play pattern is extremely limited— because of language difficulties imaginative play is non-existent and because of co-ordinational difficulties they have to be taught the necessary mechanics for riding wheeled toys and to swing, slide and climb. We teach the children to play "outdoor" games together, to run races, to play follow-my-leader, and so on, but autistic children do not understand the concept of winning and in races (whether running, hopping, swimming, or whatever) they will all wait for one another.

Indoor leisure activities for autistic children are equally limited. We provide T.V., slides, films, radio and record players. Some children look and listen, for others the appeal varies from limited interest and participation to indifference and unawareness. We teach the children to play with toys, such things as electric and clockwork trains, dolls and prams, etc., but only the most able child will extend such play to pretending the train is taking them on a journey to exciting places or that dolly is eating her breakfast, tea, etc. We teach them to play table and card games but as already pointed out the autistic child has no desire to win.

Parties, dances, concerts, are organized within the school situation, to provide opportunities for group entertainment with such activities as community singing, games and dancing and audience participation. Our children join the local club for handicapped children and attend each week—some look forward and enjoy the experience, others find the situation too demanding and have had to discontinue attendance. We celebrate as a group all functions, Easter, Christmas, individual birthdays, term parties, and so on; and thus provide experience for the give and take of sharing presents and sweets and the required good manners in such situations. We extend the child's experience to outside visits, walks, going to the shops, to parks and playgrounds, outings to the seaside, trips on the river, to suitable entertainment such as the circus, the theatre or to cartoon films and to restaurants for meals.

Obviously a great deal of adult participation is required to take our children into social situations with other children and adults, but it can be done—it may often be necessary to have a spare adult around to remove a child from a given situation in the interests not only of the child but of other people. I have found that normal society will accept so much and indeed will be "understanding" if the autistic child is small and appealing, but is less forgiving with a 13 year or older child.

Once in a while, however, despite all efforts, it is impossible to continue to include a child in wider social situations—such things as visiting a theatre, circus or restaurant. I think that after a lot of trying and failing to make such an occasion an enjoyable experience, it is kinder to the child and to other people not to include him in this kind of outing—and we make alternative provision according to the child's requirements. He may enjoy a ride in a car with a member of the staff, swimming in a pool without other children, and so on.

My house staff have the children after school from 4 p.m. on Mondays to Thursdays until 9 a.m. the following morning. Weekends are usually free but if for any reason children have to remain for a weekend I have them with me until Sunday evening and the housemothers take it in turns to come back at 6.30 p.m. If a housemother has to go out for an evening or is ill then I fill the gap.

At the Ealing School we live, work and play with the child and when he is unable to control himself we take over until he can—I try to train my teachers to foresee and avoid difficult situations but not to the extent where a child is over-protected.

The individual programmes I provide help the teacher cater for a wide range of abilities from simple skills to fuller academic activity—to cope with resistance and recognize negativism and to be able to realistically assess what the child is capable of because his development is not necessarily uniform.

At Ealing we have had our headaches and worries but no more so than in any other school, in fact probably far less than a great many.

CHAPTER 8

AUTISTIC CHILDREN AT HOME: A REVIEW OF SOME BOOKS ABOUT INDIVIDUAL CHILDREN

CHRISTINE MASON

Over the last two decades, public interest in and concern for handicapped people have grown steadily. This development has been encouraged by voluntary associations concerned with specific conditions, especially the organizations started by parents of handicapped children. One result of this increasing interest is that some of these parents have published the stories of their own children. There are now several books about autistic children, five of which will be described in this chapter.

The earliest of the five to be published, in 1960, was *Bartje, My Son* by Nel van Houten. Bartje was not classically autistic but he did have some of the features found in childhood autism, including difficult behaviour and problems with language, although he learnt to converse and even had imaginative play at a simple level. He became handicapped as a result of a severe reaction to the combined diphtheria and whooping cough immunization at 13 months of age. His story is continued up to the age of 11. Bartje's parents were Dutch but settled in South Africa after the war, before Bartje was born. He was the first of two boys.

The other four books describe children who were classically autistic in behaviour. *The Siege*, by Clara Claiborne Park, was published in 1968. Her daughter Elly at first reacted to her handicaps by extreme withdrawal and passivity and the biggest problem her parents faced was to motivate her to perform even the simplest actions of everyday living. When she did begin to make progress it was clear that she had a high level of ability in some areas, including numerical calculation. Elly's mother had measles (ordinary measles, not German measles) in the sixth month of pregnancy. Apart from this there was no known explanation for Elly's handicaps. The book describes her progress from birth until the age of 8. Her parents were both American. Elly was the fourth child in the family, having two sisters and one brother.

The Small Outsider, by Joan Martin Hundley, was published in 1971. David was an extremely difficult child, reacting to his handicaps with furious anger, temper tantrums, destructiveness and sleeplessness. During the first 6 years of David's life, which are described in the book, he remained difficult but towards the end his mother felt that he was beginning to understand more, though he still could not speak, and it was possible to introduce simple rules for him to follow. The problem of managing his behaviour was complicated by the fact that he suffered from severe allergies including asthma, skin rashes and gastro intestinal disorders. Mrs Hundley was 40 when David was born and she had much ill health during her pregnancy. David was jaundiced at birth. His parents were Australian. He was the third and youngest child in his family and had one brother and one sister.

The Fugitive Mind, by Peter Rowlands, was published in 1972. John fitted the picture of the typical autistic child almost exactly. Although he did have temper tantrums and presented many problems because of his attachment to his rituals and routines, he was less difficult than David and had a higher level of motivation than Elly. He did begin to talk but had all the characteristic problems in understanding and using speech, although he had an excellent rote memory. He learnt to read on a simple level and was good with practical tasks such as making cut-out models. No cause could be found for John's handicaps. Mr and Mrs Rowlands were English. John was the eldest of four children and had one sister and two brothers. The book describes his development from birth until 9 years of age.

For the Love of Ann, by James Copeland, was published in 1973. Unlike the others this book was written not by a parent but by a friend of the family who based his account on a diary kept by Mr Hodges, Ann's father. From birth until she was 7 years old Ann was totally withdrawn and reacted to any attempt to change her routine or to establish contact with her by wild, uncontrollable screaming. When her family found a way of helping her (described later in this chapter) she slowly began to learn social and practical skills and the basic school subjects. Apart from an incident shortly after her birth in which Ann went blue, apparently with cold, there was no known reason for her handicaps. Mr and Mrs Hodges, like the Rowlands, were English. Ann was their second child. She had one older and one younger brother. This book is the only one of the five which describes development in adolescence and early adult life. It ends when Ann was 21 by which time, although she was still handicapped, she had made remarkable progress.

In each of the families the brothers and sisters of the autistic child were normal, healthy and, at the time the books were written, apparently showed no adverse effects attributable to the presence of the handicapped sibling. Many of them were deeply attached to their autistic brother or sister and proved to be enthusiastic and successful teachers as well as amazingly forbearing companions.

The books clearly underline all the problems faced by parents, siblings, relations and friends who come into close contact with an autistic child. These problems can sometimes be noticed immediately after birth or it may take months before it becomes obvious that the child is not developing along the normal lines of infancy and early childhood. The author of *The Small Outsider* states that "No two autistic children are exactly alike in behaviour or development" and the five books confirm this point.

The realization that something is not right with the new baby usually comes first to the mother, who is in closer contact with her child than anyone else. Feeding difficulties, especially sleepiness and slowness when sucking, may be present from birth but the most worrying problem for the mother is the baby's unresponsiveness to social contact. This is very hard to put into words and when the mother reports her fears to professional workers she may be reassured and told that all will settle down in time.

Although autistic babies may show little or no interest in people they may become intensely absorbed in certain objects or visual stimuli. A carved scroll which decorated the living room wall fascinated David Hundley. Ann Hodges seemed to experience great pleasure in looking at bright lights by the time she was 6 months old. This interest in inanimate objects is in strange contrast to the disinterest in human beings which makes the parents feel that the child rejects the affection they want to give. In *The Siege* Clara Claiborne Park writes that this rejection of love is terrifying for parents, especially if it is their first child, since they have had no experience of affection from normal children and they find the behaviour bewildering. This expresses very well the feelings of distress, puzzlement and failure that parents experience during the time when they know that their child is developing abnormally but have not yet been given any adequate explanation.

In recent years knowledge of the problems of autistic children has grown rapidly. In the past, however, many parents of these children were unable to find professional workers who understood and could help. The lack of a definite diagnosis or constructive help often led to a long trail of visits to various hospitals, clinics, doctors, and therapists. Complicated journeys have been undertaken by some families, as in *Bartje, My Son*, where the mother came from South Africa to Holland in order to seek constructive help and advice for Bartje, only to meet with failure, and a long, sad return. Parents with autistic children will fully appreciate just how tiring and depressing these journeys can be.

The autistic child typically fails to respond to attempts to guide and control his behaviour. It is the mother who has to attend to the mundane tasks of running the house, undertaking the shopping, the washing and tending to the needs of the other children in the family. It is the mother who has to withstand the main brunt of a child who will not settle into any sort of routine; a child who will not respond to any attempts to set a regular feeding pattern, to toilet training, to simple commands, and who does not learn the correct patterns of accepted social behaviours which, when learnt, make life easier for everyone.

As the months pass by the strain begins to tell. In some families this can help bring all concerned into closer harmony. But this closer harmony can also bring about its own problems. Autistic children, if they cannot understand simple commands, cannot easily be left in the care of a babysitter. This means that the parents are rarely able to get away from the house together for a few hours of peace. James Copeland puts this point very well: "They lived their lives wrapped only in their little family and restricted by the walls of their tiny house." Joan Hundley writes: "The family that has an autistic child cannot live as other families do—one must stay with the small tyrant." The need for some relief for parents and siblings could be met by local groups of parents who could offer baby sitting, and by play groups with the facilities necessary to cope with several autistic children. This happens in some areas but needs to be expanded generally. The children mentioned in these books were all good looking and physically well built but their strange behaviour made them noticeable in public and occasioned disapproving remarks from strangers. How does a parent explain away head banging, spitting, ripping wallpaper, screaming, biting, rocking, smelling objects, flicking hands, spinning wheels, grabbing bright objects and removal of clothes to mention but a few of the common problems?

Sometimes the children's abnormal behaviour patterns ruled the families' lives. Strange obsessions and inexplicable fears were a feature of all the autistic children in these books. They included a fascination with lights, flicking objects backwards and forwards, intense attachment to a chair or pram, fear of open spaces, new situations, dislike of strangers and a general resistance to change. The great difficulty came when people tried to interfere with the obsessions and introduce new patterns of behaviour and new forms of occupation and interaction. It was then that frustration and temper tantrums occurred. Clara Claiborne Park felt that her daughter would only attempt new things when she thought she was not being observed and wondered whether the fear of failure might have played an important part in Elly's life.

These behaviours become harder to control as the autistic child gets older, bigger and stronger. "The difficulty lies not so much in the child itself as in one's own reluctance to be harsh with the child" writes Clara Claiborne Park. Most parents find it difficult to punish an autistic child who has no understanding of the rules of everyday behaviour and who does not know why his behaviour is considered to be wrong. In their attempts to solve the problem of how to discipline an autistic child, parents try any method they can think of and sometimes are reduced to using force. In *Bartje, My Son* the mother used physical punishment, but only in special cases of real naughtiness, when she found it effective.

In order to use punishment appropriately and effectively the parents must have a strong relationship with each other and with the child. In *For the Love of Ann* it was her father who took the all-important decision that if any improvement was to occur he would have to take a definite step to break her intense resistance to change. In Ann this resistance was particularly severe and effectively prevented her from carrying out almost all everyday activities. Ann's father eventually came to the conclusion that the only way to change her behaviour was to force her to do the things that she refused to do or appeared frightened to do. The accidental tipping of Ann's trolley which threw her on to the sand whilst on holiday started this train of thought. Ann had previously resisted being put on the sand to play and into the sea to paddle. As usual Ann screamed after the accident and was immediately returned to the trolley. Then she got herself out of the trolley and began playing with the sand and eventually the water—the first time Ann had acted as a normal child. Mr and Mrs Hodges had never used physical force or punishment with any of their children. Mrs Hodges was afraid that it would push Ann further away from them, but Mr Hodges was sure that he had found the answer that for 7 years they had been seeking. They had tried conventional methods of handling a very difficult child, but with no success. As concerned as Mrs Hodges was she agreed that they should try to eliminate one abnormal behaviour at a time with Mr Hodges actually putting the decision into effect. It was decided that instead of sitting in her rocking chair Ann should sit on a normal chair for meals and that she should be taught to feed herself. Every scream uttered by Ann was punished with a smack. In the initial stages the screaming increased but gradually the screams stopped and Ann was rewarded with social praise. With phase one of the operation accomplished, the second step of putting a spoon into Ann's hand was started. The screaming occurred again and Mr Hodges smacked Ann and repeated the procedure over and over again until Ann ceased to resist and actually began to co-operate.

The screaming and the resulting actions of Mr Hodges upset his sons and his wife at first but, as the resistance lessened in Ann, some small steps forward could be observed. On one particularly difficult occasion, after being smacked, real tears actually ran down Ann's face for the first time. During this difficult time, it was necessary to use food as a reward when Ann behaved well or accomplished a small step forward. Before her father had started this method of dealing with her, she had refused physical contact even with her parents. Gradually, however, she came to accept cuddling and eventually she enjoyed it enough for them to use cuddling as a reward. The Hodges were people who resorted to desperate measures for the love of their daughter but because their method worked with Ann it does not necessarily mean that it would work with another autistic child.

The Hodges were not trained psychologists and they had never heard of operant conditioning but, by using their own observations and knowledge of their daughter, they themselves developed methods of teaching her which were in fact the application of operant conditioning theory (see Chapter 4). It is interesting to compare the five books on the methods of teaching and behaviour management chosen by the parents.

Nel van Houten found that her version of methods she had learnt from followers of Rudolf Steiner were helpful for Bartje. These included a regular routine and teaching through drawing and painting, practical experience of materials and acting out simple stories. These worked with Bartje because he did have the beginnings of imaginative play. With the typical autistic child who lacks inner language and imagination, the fantasy would have been meaningless.

Clara Park also found that a regular ordered routine was necessary for Elly. She gradually overcame her daughter's reluctance to attempt new tasks by teaching her through bodily contact, moving her limbs through the necessary movements and guiding her from the tasks she could complete by very small steps to those she had not yet mastered. She also found it necessary to impose reasonable limits to Elly's behaviour firmly and decisively, using a slap if necessary. The prohibitions were kept to as few as possible but Elly's parents made sure that they were observed. These points are all in line with operant conditioning techniques and Mrs Park in fact recommends some reading on this subject in her book list.

Peter Rowlands does not discuss any specific techniques of behaviour management or teaching. He and his wife tried to help John by giving him as far as possible the same experiences as his normal brothers and sisters, in a simplified form where necessary. He was greatly helped by his charming and lively sister, Louise, who was about 18 months younger than John, and who understood him and tried to involve him in all her activities. Methods of managing difficult behaviour do not figure as much in this book as in the others perhaps because John was, comparatively, an easier child to live with.

Joan Hundley stands out from the other authors in that she discussed operant conditioning at length and is not at all enthusiastic about the methods or the results. She feels that the effort needed is often out of all proportion to the small results obtained and that there is a danger of turning an autistic child into a robot. On balance she seems to favour the view that autistic children should be allowed to be as happy as they can in the light of their severe handicaps and that to this end, their environment should be tailored to suit them. Some of them improve in the course of time but some do not and little can be done to help the latter group.

This is an understandable point of view. Embarking on a programme of teaching an autistic child means taking the risk that the effort will fail. However, it sometimes produces worthwhile results as can be seen from, for example, the story of Ann Hodges. Parents are entitled to know that there is no guarantee of any improvement if they try to help their autistic child by using a planned programme of teaching and behaviour management; but many decide that the risk is worth taking.

Joan Hundley is also quite right when she says that operant conditioning can be applied in a mechanical way which may do no good and possibly even do harm. It can, however, be used with sensitivity and common sense and adapted to the needs of the individual child and his family, which is how the Hodges worked with their daughter Ann. The lesson is that a programme which works with one child may be quite unsuitable for another. Attempts to take over a programme wholesale and carry it out without modification are *never* to be recommended. Autistic children are just as much individuals as any other children and should always be treated as such.

Another serious problem arising from operant conditioning is the use of ways of discouraging undesirable behaviour. As discussed in Chapter 4, it may be sufficient to ignore the child or deprive him of some object which he likes, but sometimes, as with Ann, a slap seems to be the only effective method. This is quite justifiable when it produces marked improvement in behaviour very quickly, and when social approval and disapproval are substituted as ways of controlling behaviour as soon as possible. However, if marked improvement does not occur quickly, there is clearly a danger of increasing the level of punishment beyond acceptable limits. For this reason, operant conditioning methods, when used by people professionally involved with children, should be strictly supervised by senior workers who are experienced, responsible and who have the interests of the children as the absolute priority.

Feeding problems were marked among the children described in these books. James Copeland writes of Ann's resistance to eating solid foods and her refusal to feed from any bottle except the one that was her favourite. Her parents almost found it impossible to wean her from the bottle. After many efforts they eventually managed to get Ann to eat semi-solids from a spoon but after every second mouthful she had to be given her special bottle. Mealtimes became a nightmare, a similar story to that of other parents. Bartje refused to eat solids and had to be tempted by the spoon and bottle technique after an illness at 13 months. Elly, in *The Siege,* was still finger feeding at the age of 22 months. Her mother made no great issue of teaching Elly to spoon feed herself, being content to help her with the foods that she could not grasp in her fingers.

With David, in *The Small Outsider,* early feeding appeared to be a mechanical affair. His mother would place a piece of bread in his hand and he would put it into his mouth. If he dropped the bread he made no attempt to retrieve it for himself. His mother would spoon feed him but felt that he had no great pleasure from eating. On an aeroplane flight David showed interest in food on other people's trays, snatching food as the hostess was giving the passengers their meals. He had never done this before and after the flight he made no effort to reach for food again for several years. Unfortunately during the trip David developed glandular fever and eczema. This interrupted a feeding pattern that had been established and it was diagnosed that David's body could not break down the protein in his diet. This involved a considerable amount of extra work for his mother. Milk always had to be boiled and food finely mashed and strained. If any small lumps were in the food this caused him to vomit.

David then had a severe attack of tonsillitis. He developed a great fear of swallowing and for years he was afraid whenever he saw a spoon. His mother persevered with trying spoon feeding each day but the same refusal came from David. Everything had to be strained, and his mother felt that this was not right but no one was able to give her any constructive help in breaking down this feeding pattern. Then many, many months later when his mother was making a stew David snatched a piece of potato peel and raw steak. From then on David had to taste everything he could find. By this time he was 5 years old. For a time he ate mainly raw meat, behaving rather like a young puppy. Gradually this gave way to being interested in cooked food on plates. He would allow a few spoonfuls of food to be put into his mouth, and then he began discriminating between foods he liked and those he did not like.

This interest in chewing and eating had its drawbacks because everything that came within reach had to be sampled, including broken glass, nails, gravel, plants, snails, etc. Help was given by a therapist who suggested that David should have his mouth kept full with a breakfast cereal—approximately every 20 minutes—but of course there were times when David outwitted his mother. Why was there this sudden interest in food after so many years of despairing attempts to cajole him to eat? I do not think anyone could give an accurate answer. Perhaps if his mother could have had consistent help in the early months of the feeding problem a solution might have been achieved sooner without so much distress and extra work for her.

On many occasions autistic children have been thought to be deaf and have even been diagnosed as deaf, although their parents know that they respond to certain sounds. Some autistic children react better to music than to speech and have even been taught to speak through singing. In *The Fugitive Mind* it was apparent that at an early age John was able to be calmed by music on the radio, or records, or singing by his parents. At 18 months he would sing, wordlessly, but exactly in tune. John's family were given an old piano and his mother played nursery rhymes which John would try to play for himself. He began to listen to records of music in foreign languages with rapt attention. Louise his sister could comprehend the story told in the records by studying the pictures on the record sleeves. John was content to listen to the sounds without any attempt to derive meaning. However, he did begin to sing the words of the songs as well as the tunes. One day, when having a piggy back with his mother who was repeating a rhyme, John actually joined in two lines. His father writes, "It doesn't sound much, but it was wonderful."

David in the *Small Outsider* was humming to nursery rhymes at the age of 8 months and by 12 months could hum several complicated passages of classical music, but within the next year this disappeared. Every now and again David would repeat a word after his mother. Sometimes it would take weeks for the words to come out. It was not until after David's fourth birthday that he spoke spontaneously. His mother was trying to get David into the house as it was bedtime and David said "No, No", copying his mother's tone of voice. Joan Hundley writes "Without meaningful speech the child has no interchange of ideas with others. He stays in a mental rut."

The parents of all the five children worked hard on the task of trying to improve comprehension and use of speech. In some cases the brothers and sisters joined in with equal determination. Various simple teaching methods were used, such as repeating the names of everyday objects as the child was taken round the house, varying the tone of voice to find one to which the child would respond. Additional communication through touch and simple gesture helped the learning process. Simple rhymes involving touching and naming of body parts proved especially enjoyable and useful for the child. The parents also used old magazines with pictures of everyday objects as well as the actual objects for naming. Some made models of letters in clay, plasticine and sandpaper, to give the child a three-dimensional shape to feel. In *Bartje, My Son* the mother found the best way of teaching Bartje was to draw pictures herself and interest her son in this way. The same technique was used in *The Siege* where Elly's mother drew pictures of the places where they had lived including all the items found in the various houses.

In order for a child to learn any task, no matter how simple, he must use his eyes to look at both his teacher's face and at the task material. Autistic children tend to look at both people and things very briefly, if at all, except when fascinated by something such as a piece of shiny paper. Many autistic children seem to use the senses of touch, taste and smell, rather than vision and hearing, to explore the world around them. In *The Fugitive Mind* John used his sense of touch and smell when playing with Bristol the Siamese cat. Another example was John's investigation of a new lawn mower by smelling the motor.

All these books mention the aloofness of the autistic children and the lack of motivation to indulge in any activity except their obsessional habits. It is necessary, as soon as possible, to involve autistic children in some sort of social experience outside their own homes even though they may apparently not be aware of what is happening around them. A nursery school, play group or kindergarten can be helpful if the staff are interested and willing to be patient with initial difficulties. All the books emphasize how hard it was to find suitable education for the children. In *Bartje, My Son* Bartje's mother felt very strongly that the different schools he attended had made him become personally more aware of life. In *The Fugitive Mind* John attended a kindergarten which gave him experience of the behaviour of normal children.

Most autistic children have some special areas in which they can perform at a level which contrasts with their retardation in other spheres and once these have been discovered they can make the child's life happier and more purposeful. In *Bartje, My Son* the breakthrough occurred when Bartje started to go for art lessons. These were undertaken by an art teacher who had been trained in the Rudolph Steiner techniques. The teacher and his wife were hoping to establish a pattern of work with Bartje that his own family could follow. The teacher treated Bartje as an equal and instead of wrecking the house Bartje reacted normally. The teacher and Bartje were able to become absorbed in a piece of work and all the tensions and frustrations were forgotten. Together they were achieving something which gave them both pleasure and pride.

In *The Small Outsider* Joan Martin Hundley describes not only her own experiences but also those of several other parents of autistic children. One boy, Rudy, attended school and was above average in reading and arithmetic. Fortunately, in spite of complaints about his behaviour from other parents and teachers he completed his secondary schooling. He excelled in mathematics, geography, algebra and English grammar, but fell very far behind in English expression. Unfortunately his aggressive tendencies could not be controlled and he is now in long-term care. Parents with an autistic child will appreciate how difficult it must have been for Rudy's mother to take this decision after achieving so much.

In *For the Love of Ann* it is evident that her acceptance in a school setting helped Ann to make big leaps forward in her development. She began asking questions and joining in the school's activities. There was an initial period of withdrawal but once Ann came out of this, learning became important and Ann stopped her repetitive, uncreative behaviour patterns such as rocking. When Ann changed schools to a larger establishment she showed some aggression especially in the playground and on the bus, as she was unable to tolerate the (unfortunately excessive and cruel) teasing and baiting of the other children. Reading this book gives a clear picture of how essential carefully planned educational provision is for autistic children.

Nowadays there is a growing awareness within local education authorities of the need for adequate educational placements for these children. Unfortunately financial difficulties have often delayed the opening of schools and centres. Moreover parents who live in large cities and towns are more likely to find schooling for their children than those who live in the country.

Many schools for Educationally Subnormal Children (Severe) make provision for autistic children. These schools often manage to contain and educate very difficult children to a certain level but sometimes the children's behavioural disorders can lead to suspension.

Ideally teachers should be helped and advised by psychologists and psychiatrists in the various techniques of handling the children so that the fullest possible use is made of all the potential for learning that they may have. Teachers must have a full understanding of the problems each autistic child presents and know where to get help and advice when it is needed. For a teacher working with an autistic child who suddenly makes a breakthrough and establishes a relationship, the day-to-day grind and hard work all seem worthwhile.

The effects of having an autistic child as a member of a family are almost too numerous to mention; siblings have to learn to tolerate violent outbursts shown towards them; they must put up with having their toys often broken or snatched away; families have to cope with the problems created by trying to have a holiday away from familiar settings; on top of all this they have to listen to the comments passed by neighbours, friends and relatives who fail to comprehend fully what is wrong and do not know how to deal with a child who, for example, delights in spitting straight in their eyes. Only the child's own family can really appreciate what goes on for 24 hours a day, every day of the year, year in and year out.

Parental reports and summaries are helpful as few people working with autistic children have had actual experience of living with such a child. The books express all the hopes and fears, successes and the disappointments the parents have to meet and the full emotional involvement felt by the whole family. All the children written about had differing needs, habits, obsessions, likes and dislikes, but because of the involvement of the writers it is difficult to assess the actual range of educational achievement into which these children fitted. Some obviously had more ability than others, but sometimes the ability was in one specific area only. Also the deviant behaviours mentioned were not written up systematically with all the contingencies observed and taken into account. However, despite the fact that they do not present a full and systematic account of how to manage a child with these handicaps, these books are valuable additions to the literature on childhood autism because they give professional readers an insight into the feelings of the parents in a way which no scientific account could match.

One lesson which is clear from these books is that there is a great deal of room for improvement in every aspect of the services, including adequate housing, medical diagnosis, psychological help, an appropriate educational system, provision for the care of autistic adolescents and adults and other social services which can give relief and aid to the family.

THE NATIONAL SOCIETY FOR AUTISTIC CHILDREN

The Society, which was formed in May 1962, runs an information and advisory service available to parents, workers in this and associated fields and others interested in the problem.

Five day and residential schools for autistic children have been founded and affiliated local societies have opened others. The Society encourages research into the problem and publishes a bibliography of relevant literature and many articles which will help those who wish to study the subject in detail.

BIBLIOGRAPHY

(Abbreviations as in *Index Medicus* 1973)

Anastasi, A. (1968) *Psychological Testing* (*Third edition*), Collier-Macmillan, New York.

Bartak, L., Rutter, M. and Cox, A. (1975) A comparative study of infantile autism and specific developmental receptive language disorder: I. The children, *Brit. J. Psychiat.* **126**, 127–45.

Berger, M., and Yule, W. (1972) Cognitive assessment in young children with language delay, *in* Rutter, M., and Martin, J. A. M. (eds.) *The Child with Delayed Speech*, Clinics in Developmental Medicine, No. 43, Heinemann, London.

Bettelheim, B. (1967) *The Empty Fortress*, Collier-Macmillan, London.

Brask, B. H. (1970) A prevalence investigation of childhood psychosis, Paper given at *The 16th Scandinavian Congress of Psychiatry*.

Brown, R. (1965) *Social Psychology*, Macmillan, London.

Chess, S. (1971) Autism in children with congenital rubella, *J. Autism Child. Schizophrenia*, **1**, 33.

Churchill, D. W. (1972) The relationship of infantile autism and early childhood schizophrenia to developmental language disorders of childhood, *J. Autism Child. Schizophrenia*, **2**, 182.

Copeland, J. and Hodges, J. (1973) *For the Love of Ann*, Arrow Books, London.

Cox, A., Rutter, M., Newman, S., and Bartak, L. (1975) A comparative study of infantile autism and specific developmental receptive speech disorder: II. The families, *Brit. J. Psychiat.* **126**, 146–59.

Creak, E. M. (Chairman) (1961) Schizophrenic syndrome in childhood: progress report of a working party (April, 1961), *Cerebral Palsy Bull.* **3**, 501.

DeMyer, M. K., Barton, S., DeMyer, W. E., Norton, J. A., Allen, J. and Steele, R. (1973) Prognosis in autism: a follow-up study, *J. Autism Child. Schizophrenia*, **3**, 199.

DeMyer, M. K., Churchill, D. W., Pontius, W. and Gilkey, K. M. (1971) A comparison of five diagnostic systems for childhood schizophrenia and infantile autism, *J. Autism Child. Schizophrenia*, **1**, 175.

Doll, E. A. (1965) *The Vineland Scale of Social Maturity: Condensed Manual of Directions*, American Guidance Service Inc., Minnesota.

151

Egan, D., Illingworth, R. S. and MacKeith, R. C. (1969) *Developmental Screening 0–5 Years*, Clinics in Developmental Medicine, No. 30, Heinemann, London.

Frith, U. (1971) Spontaneous speech patterns produced by autistic, normal and subnormal children, *in* Rutter, M. (ed.) *Early Infantile Autism: Concepts, Characteristics and Treatment*, Churchill, London.

Gunzberg, H. C. (1966) *The Primary Progress Assessment Chart of Social Development*, SEFA Publications, Birmingham.

Hermelin, B. (1975) Coding and sense modalities, *in* Wing, L. (ed.) *Early Childhood Autism (Second edition)*, Pergamon, Oxford.

Hermelin, B. and O'Connor, N. (1970) *Psychological Experiments with Autistic Children*, Pergamon, Oxford.

Hundley, J. M. (1971) *The Small Outsider*, Angus and Robertson, London.

Itard, J. M. G. (1962) *The Wild Boy of Aveyron*, trans. by G. and M. Humphrey from original edition of 1894, Appleton-Century-Crofts, New York.

Kanner, L. (1943) Autistic disturbances of affective contact, *Nerv. Child*, 2, 217.

Kanner, L. (1973) *Childhood Psychosis: Initial Studies and New Insights*, Winston, Washington.

Lotter, V. (1966) Epidemiology of autistic conditions in young children. I. Prevalence, *Soc. Psychiatry*, 1, 124.

Lotter, V. (1967a) Epidemiology of autistic conditions in young children. II. Some characteristics of the parents and children, *Soc. Psychiatry*, 1, 163.

Lotter, V. (1967b) *The Prevalence of the Autistic Syndrome in Children*, Ph.D. Thesis, University of London.

McDougall, J. and Lebovici, S. (1969) *Dialogue with Sammy*, Hogarth Press, London.

McNeill, D. (1966) Developmental psycholinguistics, *in* Smith, F., and Miller, G. A. (eds.) *The Genesis of Language*, M.I.T., Cambridge, Mass.

O'Gorman, G. (1970) *The Nature of Childhood Autism*, Butterworths, London.

Park, Clara Claiborne. (1968) *The Siege*. Colin Smythe, Gerrards Cross.

Pronovost, W., Wakstein, M. P. and Wakstein, D. J. (1966) A longitudinal study of speech behaviour and language comprehension of fourteen children diagnosed as atypical or autistic, *Except. Child*. 33, 19.

Rimland, B. (1965) *Infantile Autism*, Methuen, London.

Rimland, B. (1971) The differentiation of childhood psychoses; an analysis of check lists for 2,218 psychotic children, *J. Autism Child. Schizophrenia*, 2, 161.

Rowlands, P. (1972) *The Fugitive Mind*, Dent, London.

Rutter, M. (1966a) Prognosis, *in* Wing, J. K. (ed.) *Early Childhood Autism (First edition)*, Pergamon, Oxford.

Rutter, M. (1966b) Behavioural and cognitive characteristics, *in* Wing, J. K. (ed.) *Early Childhood Autism (First edition)*, Pergamon, Oxford.

Rutter, M. (1968) Concepts of autism: a review of research, *J. Child Psychol. Psychiatry*, 9, 1.

Rutter, M., Bartak, L. and Newman, S. (1971) Autism—a central disorder of cognition and language? *in* Rutter, M. (ed.) *Infantile Autism: Concepts, Characteristics and Treatment*, Churchill, London.

Rutter, M., Greenfield, D. and Lockyer, L. (1967) A five to fifteen year follow-up study of infantile psychosis: II. Social and behavioural outcome, *Br. J. Psychiatry*, 113, 1183.

Rutter, M., Lebovici, S., Eisenberg, L., Sneznevskij, A. V., Sadoun, R., Brooke, E. and Tsung-Yi Lin (1969) A tri-axial classification of mental disorders in childhood: an international study, *J. Child Psychol. Psychiatry*, **10**, 41.

Rutter, M. and Lockyer, L. (1967) A five to fifteen year follow-up study of infantile psychosis: I. Description of the sample, *Br. J. Psychiatry*, **113**, 1169.

Sheridan, M. D. (1969) Playthings in the development of language, *Health Trends*, **1**, 7.

Tubbs, V. K. (1966) Types of linguistic disability in psychotic children, *J. Ment. Defic. Res.* **10**, 230.

Van Houten, N. (1960) *Bartje, My Son*, Hodder and Stoughton, London.

Williams, P. and Kushlick, A. (1969) *Interview Schedule for Social Assessment of Mentally Handicapped Children*, Wessex Research Project in Mental Handicap (unpublished).

Wing, J. K. (1966) Diagnosis, epidemiology, aetiology, *in* Wing, J. K. (ed.) *Early Childhood Autism (First edition)*, Pergamon, Oxford.

Wing, J. K., O'Connor, N. and Lotter, V. (1967) Autistic conditions in early childhood: a survey in Middlesex, *Br. Med. J.* **3**, 389.

Wing, L. (1969) The handicaps of autistic children—a comparative study, *J. Child Psychol. Psychiatry*, **10**, 1.

Wing, L. (1970) Observations on the psychiatric section of the "International Classification of Diseases" and the "British Glossary of Mental Disorders", *Psychol. Med.*, **1**, 19.

Wing, L. (1971) Perceptual and language development in autistic children: a comparative study, *in* Rutter, M. (ed.) *Infantile Autism: Concepts, Characteristics and Treatment*, Churchill, London.

Wing, L. (1972a) *Autistic Children*, Constable, London.

Wing, L. (1972b) What is an autistic child? *Communication*, **6**, No. 2, 5.

Wing, L. (1974a) A study of language impairments in severely retarded children, *in* O'Connor, N. (ed.) *Language, Cognitive Deficits and Retardation*, Butterworths, London.

Wing, L. (1974b) *M. R. C. Social Psychiatry Unit Schedule of Children's Handicaps, Behaviour and Skills* (unpublished).

Yule, W., Berger, M., Butler, S., Newham, V. and Tizard, J. (1969) The WPSSI: an empirical evaluation with a British sample, *Br. J. Educ. Psychol.*, **39**, Part 1, 1.

INDEX

155